Junior Genreflecting

Junior Genreflecting

A Guide to Good Reads and Series Fiction for Children

WITHDRAWN

Bridget Dealy Volz

Cheryl Perkins Scheer

Lynda Blackburn Welborn

2000

Libraries Unlimited, Inc.

Englewood, Colorado

Libraries Unlimited, Inc.
P.O. Box 6633
Englewood, CO 80155-6633
1-800-237-6124
www.lu.com

Library of Congress Cataloging-in-Publication Data

Volz, Bridget Dealy.
    Junior genreflecting : a guide to good reads and series fiction
for children / Bridget Dealy Volz, Lynda Blackburn Welborn, and
Cheryl Perkins Scheer.
       p. cm. -- (Genreflecting advisory series)
    Includes indexes.
    ISBN 1-56308-556-9
    1. Children's stories Bibliography. 2. Children's stories--
Themes, motives. 3. Children's stories--Stories, plots, etc.
4. Children's literature in series Bibliography. 5. Children--Books
and reading. 6. Literary form. I. Scheer, Cheryl Perkins. II. Welborn,
Lynda Blackburn. III. Title. IV. Series.
Z1037.V66 1999
[PN1009.A1]
016.813009'9282--dc21   99-38135
                                         CIP

First and foremost, my husband, Ed;
and my family, Barbara Dealy, Katy Dealy, and Tony Gottlieb;
and in memory of my father and sister, Kenneth Dealy and Mary Dealy Urich
Bridget Volz

Maurice and Gilda Perkins,
and for my one and only, Bill
Cheryl Scheer

To my parents, Cortie and Louise Blackburn,
and to my sister, Patricia
Lynda Welborn

Contents

Preface

Genre readers everywhere are forever grateful to Betty Rosenberg and Diana Tixier Herald for creating sources that identify exactly the type of books they are craving: genre fiction. First of all, Betty Rosenberg provided easy access to genre fiction in the first three editions of *Genreflecting*. Then Diana Tixier Herald continued and expanded this fantastic idea with the fourth and fifth editions of *Genreflecting*, and reached an entirely new audience of younger readers in *Teen Genreflecting*. These two authors have made one of the most rewarding parts of reference work much easier for professionals: identifying that perfect type of fiction, or the author who writes it, and arranging it in an easy-to-use subject format for dedicated genre fans.

The books included in *Genreflecting* and *Teen Genreflecting* are exactly what genre readers are seeking. They are the ones that supply those guilty pleasures when someone reads novels for escape, for the intrigue of a mystery or the supernatural, or for just plain fun. Betty Rosenberg described it well in her introduction to *Genreflecting*:

> The reading of genre fiction is an escape into fantasizing. The reader identifies with the hero or heroine, vicariously, in a daydream, sharing adventures—physical, romantic, intellectual—quite beyond the grasp of reality but not beyond the imagination. The reader may then live in different countries, historical times, or even other worlds, entering into a society and meeting persons impossible to know or see otherwise. Or it may be fantasy of a familiar world, but still one providing experiences dreamed of but outside the realm of possibility or probability for the reader.

This not only describes what genre fans are looking for, but also describes another audience just waiting to find those special books, and that is younger readers. Children in the third through eighth grades love to read genre fiction just as much as older readers, and this book was created for those readers.

I want to thank the following people who spent countless hours making this book a reality. First of all, thanks to Lynda Welborn and Cheryl Scheer, who read and reviewed so many books, helped to identify the audience for this book, and gave the book its substance and direction. I want to thank Kim Dority and Susan Zernial for their patience, encouragement, and perseverance. Thanks also go to Stephanie Peterson for all of her advice and guidance throughout the process. This book couldn't have moved forward without the help of the Denver Public Library, particularly the Park Hill branch, for helping to find and gather all the material. A major thank-you goes to the entire student body of Colorado Academy for their insights on and evaluations of the books. Cheryl, Lynda, and I would all like to thank our families for their constant support and belief in our cause. Finally, I would especially like to thank my husband, Ed, for always listening, recommending, cooking, and being my very best friend throughout this entire process.

Bridget Volz

Introduction

The primary objective in any book about children's fiction is to provide easy access to the wealth of reading possibilities that are available for young people. Teachers and librarians all wait for the moment when a child asks for a good book to read, when they can suggest just the right book to spark that reader's interest. Our goal today is exposing children to the habit of reading and establishing a familiarity with the reading process so that every young person incorporates this habit into his or her daily life. Reading is so vital to individual growth in today's society that it is of the utmost importance to establish it as early as possible. We hope to encourage children to get excited about reading, so that it becomes not only an attractive option but also a favored choice from the smorgasbord of activities available to young people today. A perfect world would have children reading only award-winning fiction and other exceptional literature—but laying the groundwork for this type of reading opens the door to all sorts of possibilities for young readers. The books don't necessarily have to be great literature, but they should provide a time when the reader can relax, take a step back from the daily grind of life, and slip into the world of fun and imagination, where the choices are (and should be) limitless and the usual boundaries no longer exist.

Purpose of *Junior Genreflecting*

Junior Genreflecting was written to help teachers, librarians, and anyone else working with young people find the perfect books of fiction in a particular genre that will interest their readers. The books reviewed here represent the best and the most popular children's fiction published in the United States since 1990. The fiction titles included here will appeal to children who like fiction based on a particular subject but who are not necessarily looking for similar storylines or characters in each book. Popular paperback series, in which young people follow the same characters or situations as the story builds in each successive novel, are also included.

Selection of the Titles

The books that are reviewed were selected in a number of different ways. The individual titles were either selected from positive reviews in at least one of the four noteworthy publications that review children's literature (listed below), or they were taken from the annual American Library Association's notable books for children and best books for young adults lists. However, not every book that was recommended in one of these places since 1990 was included in this source, either because the reviewers felt that the age level was inappropriate for this particular resource, or because the book itself didn't belong in one of the genres being discussed.

The journals consulted in selecting the books were:

- *Booklist*, the American Library Association
- *Bulletin of the Center for Children's Books*, University of Chicago
- *Horn Book Magazine* and *The Horn Book Guide to Children's and Young Adult Books*, Horn Book, Inc.
- *School Library Journal: The Magazine of Children's, Young Adult and School Librarians*, Bowker Magazine Group

The suggestions for series fiction are based on discussions with public and school librarians, bookstore staff in children's departments, and recommendations from children. Every effort was made to include the best and the most popular children's fiction published in the United States over the past decade and to include books that are available either in bookstores, in libraries, or through interlibrary loan throughout the country.

Audience and Materials Evaluated

The primary audience for the books discussed here comprises children reading at the third-grade through the eighth-grade levels. We tried to include many bits of information that might be useful when evaluating books to purchase for the collection or for recommendation to a reader:

- We have indicated the appropriate age level for the material being reviewed and noted when the books are appropriate for older readers and when they may be too sensitive or too advanced for a younger audience. Picture books for older readers are useful when studying more difficult subject matter such as the Holocaust or the Los Angeles riots, because the stories, combined with the illustrations, are often great for initiating group discussions.

- We have included an icon designating books especially suitable for grades six to eight (**6-8**) and one for picture books for older readers (**PB**). The entries without icons are suitable for third to sixth grades.

- We have included the number of pages in each book, in case this information is necessary for school assignments.

- We have listed the ISBN number for the hardback copy that was used to evaluate the material. Be sure to check for other ISBN numbers when ordering copies of these books, because many of them are now available in paperback.

- We have included the other titles if the book being reviewed is part of a series or has a companion novel. The reviewed books were published since 1990 and may not be the first in their series, but the order in which the books were meant to be read is always listed at the end of the annotation.

- We have listed any awards that have been given to each reviewed book.

Conclusion

Lynda, Cheryl, and I have tried to be as thorough and informative as we could while pulling together this information. I'm sure that some important titles and awards may have slipped through the cracks, but we gave this our best shot and hope that it will be a valuable resource for everyone who wants to introduce these wonderful books to young people. Many new books and series are being published every day and some have already moved to the Top Ten list in popularity for many young readers. When professionals want to know the best new material that is available, they should be sure to ask the young readers. Somehow, they're the ones who always seem to know, and they love to be asked.

Happy reading,

Bridget Volz

Chapter 1

Reading for Life

The summer after my freshman year in college, I worked as a waitress in a break-fast restaurant to save some money for the following year. I often waited on two men who would take a break from their jobs to get a quick breakfast. I still remember their names, Carl and Ron, because their names were sewn onto the uniforms they wore for their jobs. The two of them always had fairly general requests and I never thought much about it until the day I served them the wrong meals. That was the moment I realized that these two men, both probably in their early thirties, had never read the breakfast menu! All that summer they had been ordering their breakfasts from the pictures on the menu, never reading what was actually included in each order. They called me to their table that morning and pointed out that the picture they had wanted on the menu was not the meal they had received. When I pointed to the written listing of their order, they ignored the printed information as though it were a foreign language, and returned to the picture of what they had wanted.

I had read about illiteracy in our society and was certainly aware of the problem in theory, but this was the first time I had actually experienced it in my daily life. I realized then that those pictures weren't on the menu purely for aesthetics or promotion; they were there to guide the illiterate sector of society in performing the supposedly easy task of ordering a meal in a restaurant. This incident was partly a reflection on my limited experience in the real world, but it has stayed with me over the years, as a concrete example of the very real learning disabilities that so many people constantly struggle to overcome or to work around in their daily lives. Because of Ron and Carl, I began to understand how not being able to read limits lives and the opportunities available for so many. I thought everyone should be able to participate in the rich world of reading that had always been such a large part of my own life. It was something I believed in, that was a part of me, and that I thought should be a part of everyone else's life. Unintentionally, Ron and Carl pointed the direction my life would take: encouraging reading as a part of life for everyone. What better way could I do this than to ignite the fire and the habit of reading in young people as early as possible in their lives?

Genre Fiction for Young Readers

Genre fiction for the young is almost the same as for any other age group, except that it is narrower in scope and in the number of genres available. Children, like adults, enjoy reading adventures, fantasies, science fiction, historical fiction, mysteries, and stories about contemporary life. Genre fiction for children doesn't usually include romance, because the interest isn't there yet, but many of the books on friendship and school (listed in Chapter 4 on contemporary life) include hints of relationships that are beginning to develop. The Anastasia series, by Lois Lowry (see page 70), and the Bingo Brown series, by Betsy Byars (see page 40), are two excellent examples of romance in the making.

Like adults, children want to read genre fiction for entertainment and relaxation. For a time, they want to escape the drudgery and the times of uncertainty in their daily lives. They want to take a break from their own routine and slip into someone else's experience, or into another world that is totally different from their own. If young people are happy and secure reading some not-quite-so-monumental fiction, isn't that better than not reading anything at all? This has long been a point of contention for many professionals in the field. My personal feeling has always been to encourage the reading of anything that piques the interest of the young person; after the habit of reading has been established, the good books, if they are available and presented in a positive, enthusiastic way, will naturally follow. *Booklist* recently carried an interview with Gary Paulsen (*Booklist*, vol. 96, no. 9/10, Jan. 1 & 15, 1999). His description of his introduction to reading matches the way I have always felt it should be:

> I grew up in a small Minnesota town. I was an "at risk" kid as they are called now, and a poor student. I actually flunked the ninth grade. And I was not a good reader. I only remember one book, I think it was called *King of the Wind*. It had a picture of an Arabian horse on the cover. Anyway, I sold newspapers at night in bars, and I found if I let the drunks get a little drunker, I could get a little more money for my papers. Instead of a dime, I could get a quarter. One winter night while I was waiting for the people in the bars to get a little more lubricated, I went into the library to get warm. That's all I went in for.
>
> The librarian asked me if I would like a library card. I was a real cocky kid, and I said, "Sure, why not." So she gave me a card, and the most astonishing thing happened. This silly little card with my name on it gave me an identity I had not had. I felt I had become somebody.

When Paulsen was asked about that librarian, he remarked that she had been old and had died while he was in the Army. He went on to say:

> But she gave me a book. At the time, nothing [in my life] was good for me: we lived in this grubby apartment building, my folks were drunks. I was sleeping in the basement on an old couch, and I was flunking school. But over the course of two years, she got me reading. I can't even imagine what would have happened to me without her. First it

was a book a month, then a book every three weeks. Eventually it was two books a week. I would get Zane Grey westerns or books by Edgar Rice Burroughs, and she would slip in a Melville or a Dickens, or something. When I brought them back, she would ask me what I thought. It was incredible.

We hope this book will generate the same kinds of feelings about books and reading in young people. There are all sorts of books listed under each genre, books that will be fun, or sad, or a little bit scary for kids, and there just might be the ones that will make a difference in their lives.

Establishing the Habit

Paperback Copies in the Collection

Like young adults, children love to have paperbacks when they read. Publishing companies are working very hard to target younger audiences and market books in exciting, attractive, and "cool" ways. The ISBN numbers listed for the books reviewed in *Junior Genreflecting* are for the original hardcover copies that were published in the United States. When putting together added copy requests or ordering new titles, be sure to check for paperback copies of the books, because those will be the most popular.

Another effective way to look for good books to buy as paperbacks is to check the *Horn Book Guide* that is published twice a year. This guide is an annotated list of "all books" published in the United States for young people during the past six months. The books are arranged by subject for fiction and in Dewey order for nonfiction. The material is rated 1 to 5, with 1 indicating the best books published during that time period. The "1" and "2" books are highlighted in the margins for easier identification. Because the material listed in the *Guide* is six months old by the time the material has been accumulated, and then ages another three to four months while the *Guide* is being readied for publication, it is the perfect source for checking on books that might have been missed in the original order, or to see if some of the books are now so popular that additional paperback copies are needed to meet the demand. Paperback purchasing is not only an effective way to evaluate the collection, but also a fine way to buy more books for substantially less money.

Reviewing Sources for New Genre Books for Young People

Journals that review children's literature specify the grade level, or the age for the youngest readers, of the readers who would most benefit from reading the books. Beyond that, the journals don't break up the fiction that is being reviewed into particular genres.

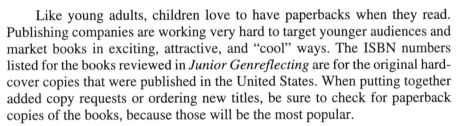
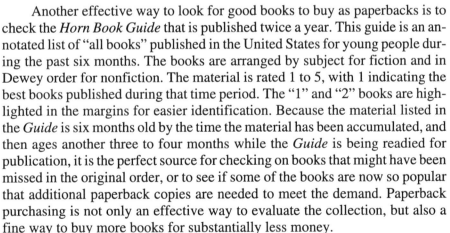
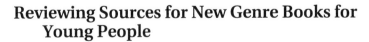

Periodically throughout the year, *Booklist* does offer various annotated lists of books for young people on certain topics, like science fiction, fantasies, or mysteries. The books included in the lists are always the scariest, most humorous, and so on, and those that are forever popular. That is, the lists are a mixture of new titles published during the past year and books that have stood the test of time and are still in demand. *School Library Journal* is another excellent source for reviews of children's materials. *SLJ* doesn't offer specific lists of books by genre, but every month it has a section devoted to new series, called "Series Roundup," to review the latest books that are available in series. *SLJ* includes both fiction and nonfiction, and it is definitely worth checking every month to stay current (maybe even ahead?) of what the kids are reading right now.

The other journals, such as *Horn Book* and *Bulletin of the Center for Children's Books*, do not separate books by genre, but they do offer informative evaluations of the books, with the genre type listed in the reviews for fiction, and the appropriate reading level.

Programs to Encourage Young People to Read

Reading has become a "cool" thing to do for many young people today. There are movie tie-ins and television programs about some popular books. This makes today an excellent time to be part of this growing movement. Making reading just as much fun as—maybe even more fun than!—media attractions has become a real challenge for teachers and librarians. This is when all the marketing skills of the professional come into play. We all have an exceptional product, the books, to sell to our audiences, and if we find winning sale approaches we can capture their attention and draw them into these funny, sad, scary, and provocative novels.

Booktalks

Booktalks have always been an effective way of enticing readers and creating demand for books. Regular booktalks are something the children can depend on and look forward to. School librarians can devote one time period a month to conducting well-advertised, much anticipated booktalks. These might start with the new books in the collection, and then alternate with booktalks on specific subjects, such as mysteries or science fiction, so that eventually the audience has a well-rounded knowledge of the entire fiction collection and some of the outstanding authors in each area.

Public librarians can offer the same type of regularly scheduled booktalks to their audiences. Advertise the booktalks heavily to the community as exciting quarterly events for specific age groups. Display the books to be presented in a highly visible area, but keep them on hold to heighten interest. Then promote the books in a lively, entertaining, can't-miss booktalk and be prepared to take waiting lists on the really popular books. Be sure to have additional paperback copies of the high-demand books, so that the young people retain their interest and don't have to wait too long. If these books become a well-known and sought-after commodity, it only increases interest, which then spills over to other books that are similar to the ones featured in the booktalks.

Discussion Groups and Genre Teams

Young people always have some thoughts on particular books, and they often can recommend other books that they enjoyed on the same subject. Allow some discussion time after the program, or schedule a time in the future when the children can offer their input on the books that were presented. This is a wonderful chance for them to shine, and it gives the librarian the opportunity to find out about the different books the children are reading and hints for new books or areas of interest that should be added to the collection as soon as possible. It also makes the library into an interactive environment where the input of every person is valid and important in shaping the collection. Some of the children might want to serve on a purchasing advisory board when orders for material are being placed.

Genre fiction can be used by reading teams either in the school or at the library. Classes can be divided up into small groups that are assigned to different genres. The children in each team put together a reading list and prepare some booktalks on their favorite books in that genre, to be presented to the class at a specific time. Then the genres can be traded as new teams are formed. The young people may even want to bring in some other forms of media that highlight some part of their genre and give their presentation a different dimension. This same idea can work in public libraries. Instead of a Great Books group, a "Great *Genre* Books" group could be formed, with different teams responsible for developing their own presentations as a part of the booktalk program. These programs not only promote the various subject areas in the collection, but also get the children involved in goal-oriented teamwork. They'll develop their own presentations on a subject in which they have developed a strong knowledge of the material. Then they will sharpen their public speaking skills when they make their presentations to an audience.

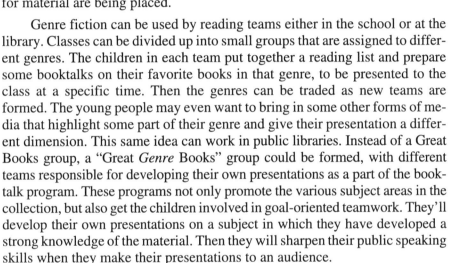

Summer Reading Programs

Libraries across the country have a history of offering excellent summer reading programs for children; these programs are usually very popular and are well received by the communities. Check with your local library and see what kinds of programs it has. The libraries set these up to motivate young people to read, so a prize is usually offered for the most number of books read or the most time spent reading. These summer programs aim to keep children in touch with their already established reading habits. They also offer quite a few other fun things to do, such as hearing speakers, listening to storytellers, doing plays or some readers' theater at the library, making craft projects, and participating in games or activities days.

Author Visits

Authors make visits all over the country to promote their books. Normally, the cost for bringing in an author will be too high for an individual school or library, but if the visit can be worked in as part of a promotional tour the author is already taking, the price can be cut down considerably. Check the authors' Web sites and find out if they are scheduled to visit somewhere close to your town, or call the authors' publishers to check the authors' fees and the possibility of a visit. Another option is to work with another group to see if the expense of bringing in an author can be split. Schools and libraries that share expenses of an author visit can have the author make appearances at both places. Two different libraries can share expenses, and bringing in the local bookstore can benefit everyone involved. Don't forget the friends' organizations that support the libraries: they are almost always interested in promoting a worthwhile project for children and books. If enough groups can work together, an author visit can become a reality in your area.

Helpful Resources for Working with Young People

I consulted the following books and bibliographies while working on this book, and I recommend them to those who are developing their own collections.

Ammon, Bette D., and Gale W. Sherman. *Worth a Thousand Words: An Annotated Guide to Picture Books for Older Readers*. Libraries Unlimited, 1996.

Berman, Matt. *What Else Should I Read?: Guiding Kids to Good Books.* Vols. 1 and 2. Libraries Unlimited, 1995 and 1996.

Colborn, Candy, ed. *What Do Children Read Next?: A Reader's Guide to Fiction for Children.* Gale Research, 1994.

Cooper-Mullin, Alison. *Once Upon a Heroine: 450 Books for Girls to Love*. Contemporary Books, 1998.

Cullinan, Bernice E. *Literature and the Child.* Harcourt Brace College Publishers, 1994.

Dodson, Shireen. *100 Books for Girls to Grow On*. HarperCollins, 1998.

Donavin, Denise Perry, ed. *Best of the Best for Children: Books, Software, Magazines, Videos, Audio, Toys, Travel*. Random House, 1992.

Estes, Sally, ed. *Popular Reading for Children III: A Collection of Booklist Columns.* Booklist Publications (American Library Association), 1992.

Freeman, Judy. *More Books Kids Will Sit Still For: A Read-Aloud Guide*. Bowker, 1995.

Gillespie, John T., ed. *Best Books for Children: Preschool through Grade 6.* 6th ed. Bowker, 1998.

Gillespie, John T. *Juniorplots 3: A Book Talk Guide for Use with Readers Ages 12–16.* Bowker, 1987.

Gillespie, John T. *Middleplots 4: A Book Talk Guide for Use with Readers Ages 8–12.* Bowker, 1994.

Gillespie, John T. *The Newbery Companion: Booktalks and Related Materials for Newbery Medal and Honor Books*. Libraries Unlimited, 1996.

Hearne, Betsy. *Choosing Books for Children: A Commonsense Guide*. Delacorte Press, 1990.

Lewis, Valerie V. *Valerie and Walter's Best Books for Children: A Lively, Opinionated Guide*. Avon Books, 1998.

Lipson, Eden Ross. *The New York Times Parent's Guide to the Best Books for Children.* Times Books, 1988.

Miller-Lachmann, Lyn. *Our Family, Our Friends, Our World: An Annotated Guide to Significant Multicultural Books for Children and Teenagers*. Bowker, 1992.

Nilsen, Alleen Pace, ed. *Your Reading: A Booklist for Junior High and Middle School Students.* National Council of Teachers of English, 1991.

Paulin, Mary Ann. *More Creative Uses of Children's Literature.* Library Professional Publications, 1992.

Silvey, Anita, ed. *Children's Books and Their Creators.* Houghton Mifflin, 1995.

Sutton, Wendy K., and the Committee to Revise the Elementary School Booklist, eds. *Adventuring with Books: A Booklist for Pre-K–Grade 6.* Bowker, 1997.

Useful Sites on the Internet

New Web sites appear on the Internet every day. At the same time, other Web sites disappear, due to lack of funding, personnel shortages, or a lack of interest by the public. Because this is such a volatile marketplace, this list includes a few major sites that are well-designed and have been reliable over time. Links to other valuable sites are included in each of these sites and are certainly worth viewing when they point to a particular subject matter of interest. Hot-off-the-press books and series are listed on the Web, along with sample chapters of some of the books, schedules for author tours around the country, and even chat rooms where young people can go and discuss the latest books written by a particular author. The material available on the Internet is endless and definitely worth the time it takes to conduct a few searches. The following tried-and-true Web sites are a good place to begin.

http://www.ala.org/alsc/ The American Library Services to Children (ALSC) division of the American Library Association has created this wonderful Web site packed with material. It includes information about various awards, the current and previous award winners, and the honor book winners for current and past years for the following awards:

- The Newbery Medal—awarded since 1922 to the author of the most distinguished work of fiction for children that was published in the United States during the previous year.

- The Caldecott Award—awarded since 1938 to the illustrator of the most distinguished picture book for children published in the United States during the previous year.

- The Mildred L. Batchelder Award—awarded since 1966 to a children's book publisher for publishing the most outstanding book in the United States that was originally published in a foreign language in a foreign country during the previous year.

- The Pura Belpré Award—established in 1996 and awarded to a Latino/Latina author and illustrator whose work was published in the United States during the previous year and celebrates the Latin culture.

- The Coretta Scott King Award—1999 marks the thirtieth year for this award, which honors African American authors and illustrators for outstanding contributions to children's literature and work toward the realization of Martin Luther King, Jr.'s American Dream.

There are also lists of the Notable Books selected by the ALSC for the current year and the three previous years.

The ALSC home page has a section called "Publications & Products." This part of the home page offers a section entitled "Reading Lists," which offers a number of links to specific sites of noteworthy bibliographies and resources, such as Vandergrift's Children's Literature Page, Carol Hurst's Literature Page, the Children's Literature Web Guide (see below), and many more.

http://www.ala.org/alsc/children_links.html The ALSC has developed an excellent Web site called **Cool Sites for Kids**. This invaluable resource includes information on "Reading and Writing," "Facts and Learning," and "Just for Fun." The "Reading and Writing" section lists the home pages for several popular authors writing children's fiction today, and their scheduled tours around the country. It also gives the Web sites for popular series, including Animorphs, The Baby-Sitters' Club, Goosebumps, and The Redwall series, to name a few. The section on "Facts and Learning" includes information on various nonfiction topics ranging from mathematics to the White House. The presentation of the material in this site brings the subject matter to life for the users. The section entitled "Just for Fun" lists several sites for games that can be played online.

http://www.acs.ucalgary.ca/~dkbrown/index.html The Children's Literature Web Guide is supplied by David K. Brown at the University of Calgary. It is definitely a useful Web site for any teacher or librarian working with children because of the amount of useful information available there. There is a section called "What's New," a list of award winners, and a list of the best books for children published during the previous year. It also links users to other Web sites for authors, professional organizations, and resources for parents and teachers.

http://www.cbcbooks.org The Children's Book Council is a nonprofit trade association of children's book publishers. The CBC site offers useful and timely information for and about publishers, teachers, librarians, booksellers, parents, authors, and illustrators. Each page offers links to new and useful information. Some of the subjects include rotating bibliographies on various subjects in children's literature; information on upcoming events, such as National Children's Book Week and scheduled author and illustrator visits around the country; important authors and illustrators everyone should know; and pertinent information on choosing books for children.

http://www.library.vanderbilt.edu/law/acqs/pubr/child.html **The Children's Literature Publishers** is a directory of publishers and vendors working with children's books. This alphabetical listing offers links to all the various publishers and vendors. The links can be searched to find out the services that each company offers and a list of titles it currently has in inventory.

These are the Web sites I like to use when looking for information on children's books. They are a great starting point for finding material on the Web and offer many links to other sites—but they are merely the beginning. Think about all the information available from individual publishing companies, from online bookstores like Amazon.com, from actual bookstores in cities around the country that have their own Web sites … The ways to find worthwhile information on the Net are endless, mind-boggling, and pretty exciting when you stop to think about it!

Chapter 2

Adventure

Adventure or survival fiction makes great reading for young readers who are looking for a good, engaging story. This genre is filled with plot-driven stories that are both straightforward and uncomplicated. They involve a protagonist who is battling either against nature or against some negative element in society, or who is on a quest to accomplish a defined goal. Historically, adventure stories have portrayed a young boy whose wits, strength, and knowledge are pitted against the antagonist who drives the plot line. The role of the hero has grown in this century to include girls who are facing the same kinds of struggles, as society has changed to reflect equal rights for women and to recognize able women and girls as credible role models. The protagonists fight the elements by themselves or with a friend, but usually without the assistance of any adults. The stories move quickly, and the question of who will survive and be the victor is never answered until the exciting climaxes are reached at the conclusion of these formulaic but riveting page-turners.

Aiken, Joan
Cold Shoulder Road

Delacorte Press. 1995.   ISBN: 0-385-32182-1. 283 p.

Arun and Is are cousins who are looking for Arun's mother. Arun's parents were members of the Silent Sect, a society in which members are not allowed to speak. Because of this stifling rule and Arun's unwillingness to join, he ran away from home. Now, a dishonest and greedy leader has taken control of the Silent Sect, and serious robberies have been occurring since the opening of the Channel Tunnel. Is and Arun are off on a series of riveting adventures, as they communicate telepathically and overcome incredible odds to bring an end to the robberies. This is definitely worth the time, for those looking for adventure.

Awards: ALA Notable Books for Children, 1997

Series/Sequels: The Wolves Chronicles: *The Wolves of Willoughby Chase*; *Cold Shoulder Road*
B.D.V.

Avi is one of the most prolific and well-received authors writing children's and young adult literature today. Not only does he write a lot of material, but he also writes effectively in many different genres. His taut storylines pull readers in almost immediately, whether the stories are adventures, historical fiction, suspense, or humorous stories about contemporary life. The following two stories are Avi at his best, telling riveting adventure yarns about the sea. Readers will be mesmerized by these tales and search for more that are just as spellbinding.

Avi
Beyond the Western Sea, Book One: Escape from Home
Orchard. 1996   ISBN: 0-531-09513-4. 304 p.

The paths of parentless siblings fleeing the horrors of the Irish potato famine and the overindulged offspring of a British lord running away from home inevitably cross in Avi's nod to the Dickensian novel. With enough plot twists and despicable characters to fill three books, this novel is very entertaining; the narrative is written with style and relish and it's obvious that the author had a whale of a good time writing it. Many will find the length daunting, particularly as the characters' fates are not revealed until the book's sequel.

Awards: ALA Best Books for Young Adults, 1997

Series/Sequels: *Beyond the Western Sea, Book One: Escape from Home*; *Beyond the Western Sea, Book Two: Lord Kirkle's Money*

C.P.S.

Avi
The True Confessions of Charlotte Doyle
Orchard. 1990.   ISBN: 0-531-05893-X. 215 p.

The year is 1832, and thirteen-year-old Charlotte Doyle is returning to the United States after attending school in England for the past seven years. Now she must cross the Atlantic aboard the ship *Seahawk* to be reunited with her family. Charlotte learns that she is the sole passenger aboard the ship and that her only companions are Captain Jaggery and the rebellious members of the crew—but the ship has already set sail and it is too late for her to leave. She then discovers that the captain is a murdering, loathsome character and that the crew is planning a mutiny. Avi's strong, female character, who embarks on the sea adventure of a lifetime, will stay with readers long after they finish this book.

Awards: Boston Globe-Horn Book Award, 1991; Golden Kite Award, 1990; Judy Lopez Memorial Award, 1991; Newbery Medal Honor Book, 1991

B.D.V.

Dorris, Michael
Guests
Hyperion. 1994.   ISBN: 0-786-80047-X. 119 p.

As a young Native American boy quickly approaching manhood, Moss has more questions than answers, and is frustrated by the adults in his life who counsel patience. An unpopular invitation from strangers (dressed oddly and unable to speak the tribe's language), to share in their harvest feast, serves as the catalyst for a premature, spontaneous vision quest for Moss. While in the woods, he is joined by an unlikely ally who helps him find answers to the perplexing problem of growing up. A fine, easy-to-read survival story that would be a good read-aloud during Thanksgiving.

C.P.S.

Farmer, Nancy
A Girl Named Disaster

Orchard. 1996.   ISBN: 0-531-09539-8. 309 p.

Eleven-year-old Nhamo must escape from her village and travel to Zimbabwe to avoid being married to Zororo, a frightful man who already has two wives. Nhamo, who wants no part of this arrangement, flees her village and sets off down the river. However, what Nhamo plans as a two-day journey turns into several months on the river, as she gets off course and ends up fighting off starvation, illness, baboons, and other terrors to stay alive. This is a thrilling page-turner, as Nhamo combats nature and becomes a woman while she is lost on the river. Farmer's powerful adventure story will be cherished by many readers.

> **Awards:** Newbery Medal Honor Book, 1997; ALA Notable Books for Children, 1997; ALA Best Books for Young Adults, 1997

B.D.V.

Hobbs, Will
The Big Wander

Atheneum. 1993.   ISBN: 0-689-31767-0. 181 p.

Clay and his older brother, Mike, have been planning "The Big Wander" for a long time. Starting from their home in Seattle, they plan to spend the summer traveling the Southwest in a beat-up truck they bought for $75. They might even discover the whereabouts of their uncle, a one-time rodeo star who has vanished. When Mike decides to head for home, Clay continues the search, eventually joined by two trusty sidekicks: a faithful dog and a burro named Pal. In a rip-roaring conclusion that should satisfy readers looking for adventure, Clay finds his uncle, saves some wild mustangs, battles the bad guys, and even gets the girl.

C.P.S.

Lawrence, Iain
The Wreckers

Delacorte Press. 1998.   ISBN: 0-385-32535-5. 196 p.

Back when sailing ships were the only way to transport goods, *The Isle of Skye* sets off on a harrowing trip from England, which will ultimately be the ship's last voyage. Fourteen-year-old John Spencer finally gets to accompany his father on the voyage, but when the weather turns bad and John's father forces the crew to go on, only horrific events take place. Lights are spotted and the crew heads the ship toward what they hope is land. Instead, the ship rams into a bed of rocks, and both the ship and John's life are ripped apart. Lawrence's white-knuckle adventure about how ships were purposely wrecked so that the wreckers could steal the cargo details a powerful struggle for survival that will keep older readers riveted to the very end.

B.D.V.

Morpurgo, Michael; Michael Foreman, illus.
Robin of Sherwood

Harcourt Brace. 1996.   ISBN: 0-15-201315-6. 113 p.

The traditional legend of Robin Hood is brought to life in a new rendition with rich, challenging text and intriguing color illustrations . A new generation of readers will be enthralled with the adventures of Robin Hood, Little John, Friar Tuck, Maid Marion, and the army of outcasts of the kingdom as they fight the evil Sheriff of Nottingham and Sir Guy of Gisbourne. The oversized format, the lively story, and the mystical illustrations make this version a sure hit.

L.W.

Namioka, Lensey
Den of the White Fox

Browndeer Press. 1997.   ISBN: 0-15-201282-6. 216 p.

Samurai action heroes Zenta and Matsuzo go on yet another caper, following their adventures in earlier novels. In this tale, set in medieval Japan, the two intrepid *ronin* enter a valley where their courage and cunning serve them well against Busuke, Lord Yamazaki's abusive agent, and a duplicitous, allegedly blind ballad singer. The action is nonstop and will leave many older readers, particularly boys, exhausted but satisfied when they finally unravel the mysteries involved.

Series/Sequels: *The Coming of the Bear*; *Island of Ogres*; *Den of the White Fox*

C.P.S.

Oldham, June
Found

Orchard. 1995.   ISBN: 0-531-09543-6. 199 p.

In the overcrowded twenty-first century, people are taxed heavily for having more than one child. Ren's mother, unable to pay this fee, arranges for her eldest daughter to live with a friend. When she is dropped off in the countryside to wait for a ride to her new home, Ren is accidentally abandoned and must learn to adapt to a hostile environment. Luckily, she meets three homeless children, and together they form a lasting bond as they attempt to survive. This provocative adventure novel with a twist of fantasy will have sophisticated readers turning the pages.

C.P.S.

Gary Paulsen is a favorite of young people, no matter what the genre. Here, he demonstrates the masterful way he can tell an adventure story.

Paulsen, Gary; Ruth Wright Paulsen, illus.
The Haymeadow

Delacorte Press. 1993.   ISBN: 0-385-30621-0. 195 p.

John isn't sure that he can manage 6,000 sheep, 2 horses, and 4 dogs for an entire summer, all alone in the remote grazing area. After all, he is only fourteen. But he doesn't have a choice when he is sent to the haymeadow for the summer. From rattlesnakes, bears, and coyotes to floods, injuries, and death, this unique adventure and coming-of-age story is told with Gary Paulsen's usual style. Just when you think nothing more can happen, yet another danger peeks around the corner. But there are also the sheep, the faithful dogs, and the peace and beauty of the mountains. This story will be remembered long after the last chapter is read.

L.W.

Thesman, Jean
Rachel Chance

| Houghton Mifflin. 1990. | ISBN: 0-395-50934-3. 175 p. |

In the summer of 1940, Rachel is about to celebrate her fifteenth birthday while her brother Rider is still in the crib. Everyone is devastated when Rider, the apple of the Chance family's collective eye, is kidnapped. Rachel is certain that she knows who took Rider and why, but she's unable to convince the adults to take action. Rachel realizes that if she wants to see her brother again, she'll have to find him herself. This exciting adventure features a strong female character reminiscent of the young women in Bill and Vera Cleaver's many wonderful novels.

C.P.S.

Turner, Megan Whalen
The Thief

| Greenwillow Books. 1996. | ISBN: 0-688-14627-9. 219 p. |

Gen, a thief in the king's prison, attracts the attention of the magus who is the king's scholar. The magus needs a skillful thief to find an ancient treasure and obtain it for the king. It is said that Gen is the most skillful thief, so he is chosen to complete the task. The journey toward the treasure is the focus of this novel of adventure and intrigue, set in Greece. Its intricate and sophisticated plot will provide a satisfying challenge to very proficient readers.

> **Awards:** ALA Notable Books for Children, 1997; ALA Best Books for Young Adults, 1997

L.W.

Paperback Adventure Series

Gary Paulsen, the popular and prize-winning author of adventure novels for young adults, has written two great adventure series for his younger fans. These exciting adventure stories, each about fifty to eighty pages long, are a great introduction to the adventure genre. The books in both series are fast-paced, fun, and easy reading for the younger set.

Series: World of Adventure

Author: Paulsen, Gary

Publisher: Dell Paperbacks

Titles:
1. *The Legend of Red Horse Cavern*
2. *Rodomonte's Revenge*
3. *Escape from Fire Mountain*
4. *Rock Jockeys*
5. *Hook 'Em Snotty*

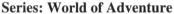

6. *Danger on Midnight River*
7. *Gorgon Slayer*
8. *Captive*
9. *Project: A Perfect World*
10. *Treasure of El Patron*
11. *Skydive!*
12. *The Seventh Crystal*
13. *The Creature of Blackwater Lake*
14. *Time Benders*
15. *Grizzly*
16. *Thunder Valley*
17. *The Curse of the Ruins*

Series: Culpepper Adventure Series

Author: Paulsen, Gary

Publisher: Dell Paperbacks

Titles:
1. *The Case of the Dirty Bird*
2. *Dunc's Doll*
3. *Culpepper's Cannon*
4. *Dunc Gets Tweaked*
5. *Dunc's Halloween*
6. *Dunc Breaks the Record*
7. *Dunc and the Flaming Ghost*
8. *Amos Gets Famous*
9. *Dunc and Amos Hit the Big Top*
10. *Dunc's Dum*
11. *Dunc and the Scam Artists*
12. *Dunc and Amos and the Red Tattoos*
13. *Dunc Undercover*
14. *The Wild Culpepper Cruise*
15. *Dunc and the Haunted Castle*
16. *Cowpokes and Desperadoes*
17. *Prince Amos*
18. *Coach Amos*
19. *Amos and the Alien*
20. *Dunc and Amos Meet the Slasher*
21. *Dunc and the Greased Sticks of Doom*
22. *Amos's Killer Concert Caper*
23. *Amos Gets Married*
24. *Amos Goes Bananas*
25. *Dunc and Amos Go to the Dogs*
26. *Amos and the Vampire*

The Authors' All-Time Favorite Adventure Stories

Farmer, Nancy—**A Girl Named Disaster**

George, Jean Craighead—**Julie of the Wolves**

O'Dell, Scott—**Island of the Blue Dolphins**

Chapter 3

Animals

Children and animals, together in a story, make up a time-tested formula in children's literature that remains forever popular with young people. The world is introduced to children by way of the animal kingdom, as they hear stories about animals, learn lessons through animals, and even watch societies develop in stories about some smart animals. Young people want to have pets of their own as they get older, not only for the feelings of love and responsibility, but also for the subtler feelings of security, familiarity, and attachment to something in their surroundings. It's a natural, then, for young readers to find both a comfort level and an attraction to reading about animals, and it is of little concern to the readers if the stories are realistic or slip into the world of fantasy. Whether children confront an issue through a pet dog or watch the mice at Redwall Abbey maintain control of their lives, the end result is still the same. The readers have a great time reading about the animals and their worlds. Here are some excellent stories that will give animal lovers some laughs, a few tears, and hours of time with the things they cherish the most.

Byars, Betsy; Doron Ben-Ami, illus.
Tornado

HarperCollins. 1996.   ISBN: 0-06-02449-7. 49 p.

A tornado is a violent storm that causes the family to go to the storm cellar. Tornado is also the name of Pete's dog from long ago. Pete, the farmhand, tells stories about Tornado that take everyone's mind off the danger of the storm. Even though Pete has told the stories many times, everyone begs him to tell them again and again. Betsy Byars's lively story is beautifully enhanced by Doron Ben-Ami's black-and-white drawings. Young readers will enjoy the tale, which is also an excellent read-aloud.

L.W.

Another excellent story by Betsy Byars, with a dog as a main character, is *Wanted ... Mud Blossom* (see page 30). This book is one of four about the delightful Blossom family. The dog, Mud Blossom, seems to be the culprit in the disappearance of Scooty, the class hamster.

Dickinson, Peter; Kees de Kiefte, illus.
Chuck and Danielle

Delacorte Press. 1995. ISBN: 0-385-32188-0. 117 p.

Chuck is one nervous whippet. She lives in constant fear that some animate (or inanimate), large (or it could be small), furry (well ... perhaps furless) THING is out to get her. Luckily, she has Danielle and her Mum to protect her from things that go bump in the night (or perhaps day). This is an unusually witty and wise dog story, told with just enough Briticisms to add flavor without putting kids off. The author is a superb writer for middle-grade readers and it's a delight to have him write for the younger crowd. Truly a joy to read.

C.P.S.

Farish, Terry
Talking in Animal

Greenwillow Books. 1996. ISBN: 0-688-14671-6. 148 p.

Siobham is an eleven-year-old with only two friends of any importance: her dog, Tree, and the woman named Maddy, a religious activist who takes care of hurt wild animals. Siobham could be content forever with her dog and her friend, but everything around her is changing. Tree is walking more slowly and dragging his feet; Maddy is protesting condom availability in the high school. Farish's novel is excellent and difficult at the same time, dealing with timely but sensitive issues. Older readers will definitely relate tearfully to the death of a pet, as well as to the difficulties faced in the adolescent years.

B.D.V.

Farmer, Nancy
The Warm Place

Orchard. 1995. ISBN: 0-531-08738-7. 152 p.

Ruva, a tiny giraffe who lives in Africa, is trapped by humans, "the sneakiest creatures alive," and taken to a zoo in San Francisco. Now Ruva must figure out how to escape from the zoo and return to her mother and to Africa—what she refers to as "the warm place." Ruva meets several animals along the way who help her with her seemingly insurmountable task. She befriends two different rats, a chameleon, and a small boy, who all work together in freeing Ruva and returning her to her home. Farmer uses her excellent storytelling skills to take middle readers on a thrilling adventure that can be read on many different and rewarding levels.

B.D.V.

Hansen, Brooks, au. and illus.
Caesar's Antlers

Farrar, Straus & Giroux. 1997.   ISBN: 0-374-31024-6. 218 p.

When Piorello, the new father of two sparrow chicks, searches for a present for his mate, he accidentally crashes through the window of Elsbeth's home, and is thought to be dead by Elsbeth's family. So begins a long period of separation for the two lovebirds. Piorello is taken to boarding school with Elsbeth, and his mate, Bette, befriends Caesar, a reindeer who is searching for the two human friends who travel with his herd. Bette builds a nest in Caesar's antlers and they join forces in their searches. The friendship and loyalty that develop between Caesar and the birds is the basis for a beautiful story about trust. Sensitive middle- and upper-grade readers will cherish this tale about love, separation, and loss.

B.D.V.

Hearne, Betsy; Erica Thurston, illus.
Eliza's Dog

Margaret K. McElderry. 1996.   ISBN: 0-689-80704-X. 151 p.

While on a vacation in Ireland, Eliza, who has always wanted a dog, falls in love with a puppy named Panda. Miraculously, her parents reluctantly agree to let her keep the dog, on condition that she take full responsibility for it. The book realistically describes the joys and anxieties associated with pet ownership as Eliza returns to her home in Chicago and takes up the daily tasks of walking and training her rambunctious friend. A cheerful, easy-to-read book that should find a ready audience with younger readers.

C.P.S.

Henkes, Kevin
Protecting Marie

Greenwillow Books. 1995.   ISBN: 0-688-13958-2. 195 p.

Fanny's dreams of owning a dog end nightmarishly. The rambunctious pup's puddles and growing pains are too much for Fanny's sixty-year-old father and she is forced to give the dog away. Months later, her father shows up with a surprise: a beautiful, full-grown dog named Marie. Although Fanny longs to love her new pet, she's also terrified that something will go wrong and her father will give Marie away. This is a wonderful novel about the complex relationship between a sensitive twelve-year-old and a temperamental parent.

C.P.S.

Jordan, Sherryl
Wolf-Woman

Laurel-Leaf Books. 1994.   ISBN: 0-440-21969-8. 162 p.

Sixteen-year-old Tanith was raised by wolves but was adopted by Chief Ahearn, whose tribe fears wolves and hunts them. As the only dark-haired person in the chief's tribe of golden-haired people, Tanith is an outsider. The lure of the wolf pack becomes stronger after Chief Ahearn is wounded and can no longer protect her. In this prehistoric setting, she must choose between the world of humans and the world of wolves. Older readers will be drawn to the story because of its rich setting, taste of romance, and the legends of the wolves.

L.W.

King-Smith, Dick; Mark Teague, illus.
Three Terrible Trins

Crown. 1994. ISBN: 0-517-59828-0. 105 p.

After the untimely deaths of her last three husbands, Mrs. Gray, the mouse, decides to devote herself to raising her three mouse sons, Thomas, Richard, and Henry, and not look for another husband. She brings up her children to have keen intelligence, an education far superior to that of normal mice, and the razor-sharp skills needed to outwit the resident cats at Orchard Farm. These capable mice do much more than rid the farm of danger. They go on to change life and society for both the rodents and the people who live at Orchard Farm, and they do this in remarkable and hilarious ways. Once again, King presents a delightful look at life where all things are possible. Younger readers will savor the antics of the Gray brothers.

B.D.V.

Knight, Dawn; Jared Taylor Williams, illus.
Mischief, Mad Mary, and Me

Greenwillow Books. 1997. ISBN: 0-688-14865-4. 95 p.

As long as Brit has lived next door to the woman all the kids call Mad Mary, she has spied on her neighbor. One day, Brit sees a dark shape through a hole in the hedge. It turns out to be a dog, something Brit has always wanted. Does the dog belong to Brit or to Mad Mary—or could they possibly share it? In this first novel, the characters are memorable and the story very satisfying. Readers can look forward to future books by Dawn Knight.

L.W.

L ois Lowry is fabulous, whether her stories concern science fiction, contemporary life, or (as here) the dog named Keeper. Be sure to look for Lowry's books in the other chapters.

Lowry, Lois; True Kelley, illus.
Stay! Keeper's Story

Houghton Mifflin. 1997. ISBN: 0-395-87048-8. 128 p.

Keeper, a dog who has learned a lot about life, has quite a story to tell about his adventures. He was born in an alley where he spent the first few weeks of his life. He was then separated from his mother and siblings, but had the spunk to make it on his own and set off to find out what life had to offer. Keeper settles in with various people, adjusts to having different names, and even becomes a highly sought-after model, but he always hopes he'll be able to track down his missing sister. Lowry gives a heart-warming account that is definitely a step above typical talking animal stories. Middle readers will be delighted by the tale, and will come away from the story with new information on the behaviors of both humans and canines.

B.D.V.

Mazer, Anne
The Oxboy

Alfred A. Knopf. 1993.   ISBN: 0-679-84191-1. 109 p.

A young boy's happy family is split up when his father's life is threatened; the father must leave his wife and child or face certain death. The boy,
who is the offspring of a union between an ox and a human woman, survives in
a society that worships purebloods and detests and exterminates mixed bloods
and animals. Although his heritage isn't apparent from his looks, the boy is finally forced to leave his home as hostile forces conspire to make a peaceful life
impossible for him. This easy-to-read examination of prejudice is for that special reader who enjoys challenging and enigmatic novels; others will be left
scratching their heads in bewilderment.

C.P.S.

McKay, Hilary
Dog Friday

Margaret K. McElderry. 1995.   ISBN: 0-689-80383-4. 135 p.

Robin, a ten-year-old who lives with his mother, has been afraid of dogs
ever since he was attacked on the beach by one. He has been working to overcome this fear when the unlikeliest family moves in next door to help him on
his road to recovery. The children earn Robin's trust and set out to introduce
him to every dog in the neighborhood. Meanwhile, Robin becomes attached to
a stray, starving dog that has been left on the beach to die; finally, Robin takes
him home. All the children work together to keep the dog, while bringing a
sense of merriment into Robin's life. This is delightful reading for any
middle-grade reader looking for a warm, entertaining story.

Awards: ALA Notable Books for Children, 1996

Series/Sequels: *Dog Friday*; *The Amber Cat* (p. 95)

B.D.V.

All three of the books in Naylor's next trilogy are just terrific! It is well
worth reading the trilogy in its entirety just to learn the outcome for Shiloh.

Naylor, Phyllis Reynolds
The Shiloh Season

Atheneum Books for Young Readers. 1996.   ISBN: 0-689-80647-7. 120 p.

Shiloh was a mistreated dog who used to belong to the town drunk, Judd
Travers. Determined to save this animal, Marty Preston managed to earn Shiloh by working at menial jobs for Judd. Now Judd has decided that he wants
the dog back, and it appears that he will stop at nothing to have his way. Shiloh
saves Judd's life after a traffic accident leaves him badly injured, and Marty
decides that perhaps by showing Judd kindness and understanding, he will be
able to heal Judd's meanness. This is the second title in this excellent trilogy.

Series/Sequels: *Shiloh*; *The Shiloh Season*; *Saving Shiloh*

C.P.S.

Oppel, Kenneth
Silverwing

Simon & Schuster Books for Young Readers. 1997.   ISBN: 0-689-81529-8. 217 p.

Shade, the newborn bat in the colony, is referred to by everyone else as "Runt" because he is so small. Shade is very smart, though, and the elders feel he has something special about him. When Shade is separated from the rest of the colony during migration, he demonstrates to everyone how brave and smart he really is. He even begins to understand the meaning of the silver ring. Oppel has created a heartwarming and believable world with bats as the characters. Middle readers won't be able to put down this exciting, fast-paced adventure, which appears to be the first in a series of many stories about Shade and his colony.

B.D.V.

Philbrick, Rodman
The Fire Pony

Blue Sky Press. 1996   ISBN: 0-590-5525-1. 175 p.

Joe Dilly rescues his little brother, Roy, from an abusive foster home, and the two of them hit the road. Because they both have a way with horses, they are welcomed to the Bar None Ranch. If Roy can break the wild pony, Lady, he can have her for his own. Maybe Joe and Roy will finally be able to settle down in one place if the secrets in their past don't catch up with them. This is an exciting story with a twist that lifts it far above the average horse story.

L.W.

Seidler, Tor; Fred Marcellino, illus.
The Wainscott Weasel

HarperCollins. 1993.   ISBN: 0-062-05032-X. 194 p.

The weasels who live in Wainscott are a happy bunch of characters. They don't have to spend their time hunting because of the handy food-gathering system developed by the famous Bagley Brown, who has since gone to his reward. All the weasels are now free to take part in their favorite pastime: dancing. Everyone in town couldn't be happier, except for Bagley Brown Jr., the son of the famous hero. Bagley Brown Jr. is sad, lonely, and of all things, in love with a fish! Young readers will cheer for Bagley Brown Jr. as he hatches a plan to save the fish from impending death. When he carries out this plan, though, could he become even more famous than his legendary father in the town of Wainscott?

If you like the way Seidler writes about animals, be sure to check out *Mean Margaret*, reviewed on page 90 in the Fantasy chapter.

B.D.V.

Walsh, Jill Paton; Alan Marks, illus.
Matthew and the Sea Singer

Farrar, Straus & Giroux. 1993   ISBN: 0-374-34869-3. 46 p.

Birdy, a young girl who lived in Scotland, saw a terrible sight when she went to town one day. The orphan master was selling children for a shilling, and a farmer wasn't paying the price for the scrawny little boy named Matthew. Birdy bought the boy on the spot and took him home to her village by the sea. The next morning, Matthew began to sing with a voice that made everyone stop to listen—including the seals. The seal queen kidnapped Matthew and agreed to return him only if one of her seal pups could be taught to sing, too. Walsh has woven a beautiful tale about human nature, the animal kingdom, and caring. Young readers will delight in the story and Marks's creative illustrations.

Awards: ALA Notable Books for Children, 1993

B.D.V.

Paperback Animal Series

Young people love to read stories with animals at the center of the action, especially horses. These series are similar in format to other series that are listed in the Contemporary Life chapter (Chapter 4), but the surroundings change to stables, ranches, and riding camps. The young characters are still working on friendships, relationships, families, and life's problems, but enhancing the storyline with the animals and horses gives the plot a different dimension. There is the added attraction of learning about horses, the excitement that goes with learning to ride, and the responsibility of caring for a horse or other animals. New series are popping up all the time and many immediately become popular. Some examples of these are the Thoroughbred series, created by Joanna Campbell; the Animal Ark series, by Lucy Daniels; and the really successful Sandy Lane Stable series, by Susannah Leigh. If a reader is interested in this genre, these definitely shouldn't be overlooked. We've also listed some tried-and-true series and the individual book titles for readers who want to be sure that they have read all the books with their favorite characters.

Series: The Saddle Club

> Author: Bryant, Bonnie

> Publisher: Bantam Books

Stevie, Lisa, and Carole are the founding members of the Saddle Club. They board their horses at Pine Hollow Stables, take riding lessons, and have become best friends. Each is crazy about horses and is committed to helping the others with any of life's problems. The Saddle Club is a well-liked series for horse lovers and for those involved in the trials of adolescence.

Titles: 1. *Horse Crazy*
2. *Horse Shy*
3. *Horse Sense*
4. *Horse Power*
5. *Trail Mates*
6. *Dude Ranch*
7. *Horse Play*
8. *Horse Show*
9. *Hoof Beat*

10. *Riding Camp*

11. *Horse Wise*

12. *Rodeo Rider*

13. *Starlight Christmas*

14. *Sea Horse*

15. *Team Play*

16. *Horse Games*

17. *Horsenapped*

18. *Pack Trip*

19. *Star Rider*

20. *Snow Ride*

21. *Racehorse*

22. *Fox Hunt*

23. *Horse Trouble*

24. *Ghost Rider*

25. *Show Horse*

26. *Beach Ride*

27. *Bridle Path*

28. *Stable Manners*

29. *Ranch Hands*

30. *Autumn Trail*

31. *Hayride*

32. *Chocolate Horse*

33. *High Horse*

34. *Hay Fever*

35. *Horse Tail*

36. *Riding Lesson*

37. *Stage Coach*

38. *Horse Trade*

39. *Purebred*

40. *Gift Horse*

41. *Stable Witch*

42. *Saddlebags*

43. *Photo Finish*

44. *Horseshoe*

45. *Stable Groom*

46. *Flying Horse*
47. *Horse Magic*
48. *Mystery Ride*
49. *Stable Farewell*
50. *Yankee Swap*
51. *Pleasure Horse*
52. *Riding Class*
53. *Horse-sitters*
54. *Gold Medal Rider*
55. *Gold Medal Horse*
56. *Cutting Horse*
57. *Tight Rein*
58. *Wild Horses*
59. *Phantom Horse*
60. *Hobbyhorse*
61. *Broken Horse*
62. *Horse Blues*
63. *Stable Hearts*
64. *Horse Capades*
65. *Silver Stirrups*
66. *Saddle Sore*
67. *Summer Horse*
68. *Summer Rider*
69. *Endurance Ride*
70. *Horse Race*
71. *Horse Talk*

The "Super Editions" are well-received spinoffs for Saddle Club fans.

Series: The Saddle Club Super Editions

Author: Bryant, Bonnie

Publisher: Bantam Books

Titles: 1. *A Summer Without Horses*
2. *The Secret of the Stallion*
3. *Western Star*
4. *Dream Horse*
5. *Before They Rode Horses*
6. *Nightmare*

Here is another popular series about horses for readers aged twelve and under.

Series: Short Stirrup Club

Author: Estes, Allison

Publisher: Pocket Books

Megan, her brother Max, and their friends Chloe, Keith, and Amanda board their horses and take riding lessons at the Thistle Ridge Farm. They formed the Short Stirrup Club because they all show their horses in the Short Stirrup Division at local horse shows. The series concerns the action-packed adventures they have with their horses and with each other.

Titles: 1. *Blue Ribbon Friends*

2. *Ghost of Thistle Ridge*

3. *The Great Gymkhana Gamble*

4. *Winner's Circle*

5. *Gold Medal Mystery*

6. *Friends to the Finish*

7. *Legend of the Zuni Stallion*

8. *Victory Ride*

9. *Playing for Keeps*

10. *Pony Express*

The Authors' All-Time Favorite Animal Stories

Fox, Paula—**One-Eyed Cat**

Menino, H. M.—**Pandora: A Raccoon's Journey**

O'Brien, Robert C.—**Mrs. Frisby and the Rats of NIMH**

Rawls, Wilson—**Summer of the Monkeys**

White, E. B.—**Charlotte's Web**

Williams, Margery—**The Velveteen Rabbit**

Chapter 4

Contemporary Life

Young people growing up in the world today are inundated with so much activity, so many events in their busy schedules. While they juggle all these school, family, and community activities, they are responsible for developing their own personalities and figuring out how they fit into the world around them. Finding books about other children who are working through similar situations can be both comforting and helpful during these sometimes stressful, lonely, and frustrating times. The children in these books face the same social situations every young person must tackle. These characters often find the humor in the juggling act they must perform to live in harmony with the other members of their families. They come to realize the importance of friendship. They get through those hilarious, embarrassing times at school. Some even deal with divorce, illness, abuse, and death. What an opportunity for kids in today's society to read about other children (even if they're only fictitious) who make it through these turbulent years! These stories take the edge off seemingly insurmountable problems; they make it possible for readers to step back and see how funny some of these situations really are. They help readers realize that they aren't the only ones who have ever experienced these circumstances. Most of all, they offer readers a chance to relax and be happily entertained, away from the pressures of their lives. These books will make some readers laugh, leave others brushing away tears, and will leave everyone thoroughly entertained.

Families and Family Life

Blegvad, Lenore; Erik Blegvad, illus.
A Sound of Leaves

Margaret K. McElderry. 1996.   ISBN: 0-689-80038-X. 58 p.

Nine-year-old Sylvie takes her first vacation to the beach. There she finds out how it feels to be away from home and living in a totally foreign environment. On the surface, Sylvie's story appears to be a simple tale about a vacation. At second glance, though, a rich story unfolds about friendship, homesickness, prejudices, and growth that Sylvie experiences through her new picture of a larger and deeper world. This story is aimed toward younger readers, but any reader can understand and identify with Sylvie in this heartfelt story about life's constant growth and change.

B.D.V.

Brooks, Bruce
What Hearts

Laura Geringer (HarperCollins). 1992.   ISBN: 0-06-021131-8. 194 p.

Four interrelated stories about Asa's life begin when he is in the first grade and end when he is an adolescent. During that time, he deals with his mother's mental illness and a strained relationship with his new stepfather, Dave. He also learns about friendship, love, forgiveness, and humor in a story that revolves around sports. The subtle depth of this novel, with its complicated themes, will give mature readers food for thought and insights into growing up in a less-than-perfect family.

L.W.

B etsy Byars develops every character, including the pets, in her wonderful series about the Blossom family. As always, Byars's understanding of family life today is right on target, and her presentation is bound to bring out the giggles in every reader.

Byars, Betsy; Jacqueline Rogers, illus.
Wanted ... Mud Blossom

Delacorte Press. 1991.   ISBN: 0-385-30428-5. 148 p.

Junior, the youngest member of the Blossom family, can't wait for the weekend to begin. He has been given the responsibility of watching Scooty, the class hamster, for the weekend, and has even built a special vacation home for the hamster in their back yard. But then Scooty disappears, and Mud, the family dog, is put on trial for murder! Scooty isn't the only character that is missing for the Blossoms. It appears that Mad Mary, the friendly but rather odd town resident who lives in a cave, is missing and may have been kidnapped. The Blossoms continue with their uproarious adventures, as Byars brings back these charming characters for one more delightful story for middle readers.

Awards: ALA Notable Books for Children, 1991

Series/Sequels: *The Not-Just-Anybody Family*; *The Blossoms Meet the Vulture Lady*; *The Blossoms and the Green Phantom*; *A Blossom Promise*; *Wanted ... Mud Blossom*

Christiansen, C. B.
I See the Moon

Atheneum. 1995.   ISBN: 0-689-31928-2. 116 p.

Twelve-year-old Bitte's sister Kari is fifteen and pregnant. Bitte is very excited about the prospect of becoming an aunt, but soon discovers that Kari is planning on giving up the baby. When Bitte's attempts to change her sister's mind only make Kari more unhappy, she is sent to live with Uncle Axel, who is grieving about his separation from his wife, Minna, who is ill with Alzheimer's disease. The lessons Bitte learns from her uncle about love and devotion help her grow up and accept her sister's decision. A wise, gentle, well-written story that many readers will enjoy.

C.P.S.

Cooney, Caroline B.
The Voice on the Radio

Delacorte Press. 1996.   ISBN: 0-385-32213-5. 183 p.

Sixteen-year-old Janie, the character who was kidnapped in *The Face on the Milk Carton*, feels that life is finally returning to normal. She does miss her boyfriend, Reeve, though, who has gone off to college and gotten a job at a radio station. What Janie doesn't realize is that Reeve's program is a talk radio show, and that he is telling the story of her kidnapping on the air to all of his listeners, even though he has been sworn to secrecy about the incident. It is well worth it for all of Cooney's fans to read the exciting conclusion to this gripping trilogy.

Awards: ALA Best Books for Young Adults, 1997

Series/Sequels: *The Face on the Milk Carton*; *Whatever Happened to Janie?*; *The Voice on the Radio*

B.D.V.

Creech, Sharon
6-8 Chasing Redbird

HarperCollins. 1997.   ISBN: 0-06-026987-1. 272 p.

When life among a herd of brothers and sisters became too much, Zinny Taylor could always run next door to Aunt Jessie's. Now her aunt has died and her Uncle Nate is dancing the boogie-woogie with an invisible partner. While seeking a solitary refuge in which to sort out her confusion about life, love, and death, Zinny stumbles upon the overgrown remains of a twenty-year-old trappers' trail and decides to clear it of weeds and debris. In the process, she manages to sort out her own tangled emotions about growing up. A fine coming-of-age novel, which girls particularly will love.

Awards: ALA Best Books for Young Adults, 1998

C.P.S.

Creech, Sharon
Walk Two Moons

HarperCollins. 1994.   ISBN: 0-06-02334-6. 280 p.

When thirteen-year-old Salmanca Tree Hiddle's mother ran away to Idaho, she promised to return before the tulips bloomed—but she hasn't come back. As Sal and her grandparents trace her mother's trip from Ohio to Idaho, Sal tells them the story of her friend Phoebe Winterbottom, whose mother also vanished. They listen to how Phoebe received messages from a "potential lunatic" whom she is sure kidnapped her mother. This story of two girls who are desperately seeking their mothers is richly layered with mystery, humor, hope, and sadness. Readers of all ages will never forget this Newbery Medal-winning story.

Awards: Newbery Medal, 1995

L.W.

Doherty, Berlie
White Peak Farm

Orchard. 1990.   ISBN: 0-531-05867-0. 102 p.

Very little changes on the Tanner's sheep farm amidst the rolling hills of Derbyshire, or so Jeannie believes—until her Gran upsets the applecart by selling all her possessions and announcing her intention to move to India. Thus begins a chain of events resulting in changes, both large and small, affecting virtually every member of the family and culminating in Jeannie herself leaving home. This poignant, beautifully written novel will attract mature readers who have the inclination to reflect on its subtle message and prose.

C.P.S.

Dorris, Michael
The Window

Hyperion. 1997.   ISBN: 0-7868-0301-0. 106 p.

Eleven-year-old Rayona spends a lot of time alone while her Native American mother has what she refers to as more "hard nights." Finally, Rayona's mother admits to having a drinking problem and seeks help. But what will happen to Rayona? Her African American father, who doesn't live with them, takes Rayona to live with his relatives, whom she has never met before. This becomes a time of realizations, of learning and of growing, not only for Rayona's mother, but also for Rayona and everyone else in this unusual family. Middle readers will become attached to these wonderful characters as they all learn to appreciate and cherish the differences in mixed-race relationships.

B.D.V.

Fletcher, Ralph
Fig Pudding

Clarion Books. 1995.   ISBN: 0-395-77125-8. 136 p.

Eleven-year-old Cliff, the eldest of six children (five of them boys), recalls the events of one year in the life of the boisterous Abernathy family. Some of these recollections are extremely funny, such as trying to decipher little Josh's Christmas wish list; others are sad, as one of the brothers unexpectedly dies. Despite all of the turmoil and feelings of being misunderstood, the common bond of love makes this family special. Some of the chapters could stand alone as read-alouds, but to get the most from this well-written novel, read it as a whole.

Awards: ALA Notable Books for Children, 1996

C.P.S.

Godden, Rumer; Ian Andrew, illus.
Premlata and the Festival of Lights

Greenwillow Books. 1996. ISBN: 0-688-15136-1. 58 p.

Every household lights *deepas*, tiny earthenware leaf-shaped lamps, for the Diwali Festival of Lights. In India, Diwali is the night when the great goddess Kali goes out to fight against the demons of evil, and thousands of *deepas* help light her way. Premlata's house will be the only one left in darkness because her mother, Mamoni, has had to sell the family's Diwali lamps to buy rice for her three children. With the help of the richest man in the village, Bijoy Rai, and Rajah, the elephant, Premlata finds a way to bring hope and light to her family.

L.W.

Hall, Barbara
Dixie Storms

Harcourt. 1990. ISBN: 152-23825-5. 197 p.

Fourteen-year-old Dutch Peyton is struggling to keep her unhappy family together. A severe drought has crippled their farming community and her father and older brother are helpless to save their tobacco crop. Younger nephew Bodean is desperately unhappy after he is apparently abandoned by his mother, and Aunt Macy is ineffectual and timid. When Dutch's attractive cousin, Norma, arrives to spend the summer while her parents settle their marital disputes, the atmosphere becomes even more explosive. This is a compelling portrait of a young woman's attempts to come to grips with change.

C.P.S.

Honeycutt, Natalie
Twilight in Grace Falls

Orchard. 1997. ISBN: 0-531-30007-2. 181 p.

Dasie Jenson has lived in Grace Falls all eleven years of her life and loves the town. The logging industry touches the lives of all of the townspeople in some way, so when the lumber mill closes, everyone is affected. Dasie can't bear the facts that people are moving away and the future looks bleak. The importance of friends and family during good times and bad is the focal point of this bittersweet story.

L.W.

Howker, Janni; Anthony Brown, illus.
The Topiary Garden

Orchard. 1995. ISBN: 0-531-06891-9. 63 p.

Ninety-one-year-old Sally Beck tells Liz, "I was a boy once upon a time." Liz is intrigued by the retired gardener and by the topiary garden at Carlton Hall. Each time she visits, Liz learns more about Sally's years when she was disguised as Jack Beck. This tiny little jewel of a book, with its unusual illustrations, will captivate American children as it did those overseas when it was published in Great Britain more than ten years ago.

L.W.

Hurwitz, Johanna; Eileen McKeating, illus.
Ozzie on His Own

Morrow Junior Books. 1995. ISBN: 0-688-13742-3. 115 p.

Eight-year-old Ozzie is sure that this will be the most boring summer of his life, because his best and only friend, Roz, is away in England. Then he meets Ryan, Ditto, Candy, and Snow White, the mouse. After they build a clubhouse, the summer definitely improves. Then Ozzie's father has a heart attack. Just when Ozzie feels completely alone, he learns that people of all ages care about him. The emotions of happiness, loneliness, and fear are intertwined in this sequel to *Roz and Ozzie*.

Series/Sequels: *Roz and Ozzie*; *Ozzie on His Own*

L.W.

Koller, Jackie French
6-8 A Place to Call Home

Harcourt Brace. 1995. ISBN: 0-689-80024-X. 204 p.

When her mother disappears, fifteen-year-old Anna is not too alarmed, despite being left in charge of her two younger siblings. Mom has frequently taken off on alcoholic binges and Anna's main concern is making sure that Social Services not be informed. However, when she discovers that her mother has committed suicide, Anna is faced with trying to hold her family together against what are, ultimately, insurmountable odds. There are several books dealing with this subject and this is one of the best. Sure to be popular with older readers.

Awards: ALA Notable Books for Children, 1996

C.P.S.

MacLachlan, Patricia
Journey

Delacorte Press. 1991. ISBN: 0-385-30427-7. 83 p.

Journey is eleven the summer his mother leaves him and his sister, Cat, with their grandparents. He searches photographs to find the reason why she left. Grandfather finds old photographs and takes new ones to prove the existence of family to Journey. In her usual spare but eloquent style, MacLachlan has written a story filled with humor and wisdom through the eyes of Journey.

L.W.

McDonald, Joyce
Comfort Creek

Delacorte Press. 1996.   ISBN: 0-385-32232-1. 194 p.

Quinnella's father has lost his job, and the family has to move to a remote place in the Florida swampland. Not getting to be the editor of her sixth-grade newspaper turns out to be the least of Quin's problems. She becomes involved in a conflict between saving the land and the prospect of new jobs when a mining company plans to move into the area. Everyone takes sides in this realistic story of a family going through hard times.

L.W.

Naylor, Phyllis Reynolds
Ice

Atheneum Books for Young Readers. 1995.   ISBN: 0-689-800005-3. 199 p.

Chrissa's heart has been like ice since her father left three years ago. Now that she is in junior high, her mother decides that the two of them need a rest from each other. Chrissa must leave New York City and go to live on her Gram's farm. When Gram is about to be swindled out of her land by the phony evangelist, Sister Harmony, Chrissa learns that she must confront the crisis herself. This heartwarming story about a young girl who discovers her own strength shows another side of its talented author, Phyllis Reynolds Naylor.

L.W.

Paterson, Katherine
Flip-Flop Girl

Lodestar. 1994.   ISBN: 0-525-67480-2. 120 p.

Daddy brought Vinnie presents, cooked her spaghetti, rocked her in the big chair, and told her knock-knock jokes. Since Daddy died of cancer, Vinnie has felt invisible. All the attention is given to her younger brother, Mason, who has refused to speak since Daddy died. To make matters worse, they must go to live with Grandma and go to a new school where people tease Vinnie and ask why Mason is so crazy. Vinnie notices a girl who is wearing bright orange flip-flops and playing hopscotch alone. Lupe, Mason, and Vinnie are all children who have been robbed of many of the joys of childhood, but a teacher, Mr. Clayton, provides a positive role model and brings hope to their lives.

L.W.

Patron, Susan; Dorothy Donahue, illus.
Maybe Yes, Maybe No, Maybe Maybe

Yearling Books. 1993.   ISBN: 0-440-40969-1. 87 p.

PK is stuck in the middle between her two sisters, Megan and Rabbit. Megan is almost a teenager, and mother says her extreme moods and affectations are caused by hormones. Rabbit is happiest when she is in the bathtub and PK is telling the magic stories that she finds in the old built-in clothes hamper. When they move to a bigger house, PK has to figure out a way to bring the stories with her. Each of the sisters in this short, lively story is a special character. Young readers will be delighted with PK and the rest of her family.

L.W.

Rodowsky, Colby
Hannah In Between

Troll Medallion. 1994.   ISBN: 0-8167-3740-1. 152 p.

Predictable and *comfortable* were good words to describe eleven-year-old Hannah's life. In fact, she even created the word *precomfordictable* to describe the vacation she takes to the beach every summer with her family. The summer Hannah is twelve, things begin to change. Her mother drinks too much. The mother she has always depended on becomes loud, argumentative, and forgetful. Can Hannah be the only one who notices? Rodowsky handles the problem of an alcoholic parent with skill and sensitivity. The reader is hopeful when Hannah's mother seeks help through Alcoholics Anonymous. The bibliotherapeutic message is strong in this very readable middle-grade novel.

L.W.

Family Relations

A tale about family life in general can be exactly the kind of story a young reader is trying to find. Some readers, though, are looking for that perfect story that mirrors the very situation they find themselves in at the time. They want to read about other people their age who, in their opinion, have the most difficult parents, or terrible brothers and sisters, or distant and unreachable grandparents. They need to understand how these people can be both the best and the worst human beings they have ever met; these readers want to know that they are not alone in their feelings. Many of the stories leave readers laughing about the silly situations all families get themselves into. Other stories leave the readers saddened, but feeling special because the author was willing to share those personal, innermost feelings with them. All of these stories ring true for readers who are looking for that moment of recognition and understanding, when they realize that lots of people feel exactly the same way they do about their own family members. The books listed here can give all readers a real sense of community. They show that these situations, when looked at from another perspective, can be pretty funny; or they help some readers feel safe, knowing that "misery loves company."

Fathers

Avi
Blue Heron

Simon & Schuster. 1992.   ISBN: 002-707-7519. 192 p.

Maggie is justifiably apprehensive about spending August with her dad, now that he's remarried and has a new baby girl. Right away she notices how angry her father is: he snaps at his wife, has little patience with Maggie, and pays no attention to four-month-old Linda. Maggie's only refuge is the lake in front of their cabin, made special by the beautiful blue heron living there. Tensions mount and Maggie realizes that both her father's life and the heron's are in danger—yet there's little she can do about it. The book ends with questions left unanswered as Maggie returns to her home, vacation cut short by an almost fatal car accident involving her father. This is a realistic look at a family in crisis.

C.P.S.

Hamilton, Virginia
Plain City

Blue Sky Press. 1993. ISBN: 0-590-47364-6. 194 p.

Twelve-year-old Buhlaire has spent her entire life feeling like she doesn't belong. She looks different from everyone else and she seems to have no friends. She also knows that she has a strange family that is unlike anyone else's. Her father is "missing in action"; her mother is the famous singer Bluezy Sims, who travels most of the time; and her Aunt Digna, the only constant family Buhlaire really has, may not even like her. Buhlaire convinces herself that none of this bothers her, until she receives some unexpected information about her father. Hamilton tells an engrossing story about a mixed family in which mental illness exists. Older readers will identify with Buhlaire's struggles.

B.D.V.

Salisbury, Graham
6-8 Shark Bait

Delacorte Press. 1997. ISBN: 0-385-32237-2. 151 p.

Mokes has seen much that is well beyond his twelve years, because he is the police chief's son in the small town of Kailua, Hawaii. He has seen his quiet town spark to life with activity as the Navy ships dock overnight and sailors explode into town for a night of partying, drinking, and carousing. Mokes receives very specific instructions on this day: be home by six o'clock, because a ship has come to town and trouble is expected for tonight. Mokes disobeys his father, though, and what begins as merely staying out late, to see a fight, turns into a violent struggle as a gun becomes part of the action. Older, more sophisticated readers won't be able to put down this attention-grabbing page-turner.

B.D.V.

Stepfathers

Sherman, Charlotte Watson; James Ransome, illus.
Eli and the Swamp Man

HarperCollins. 1996. ISBN: 0-06-024723-1. 90 p.

Eight-year-old Eli doesn't like his new stepfather, and he hasn't seen his real father for two years. Eli decides to run away from home and ride his bike to Alaska, where his father is now living. None of Eli's friends will ride with him, though, because Alaska is too far away, so Eli takes off on his own. He takes a shortcut through the swamp on his way out of town, and there he meets

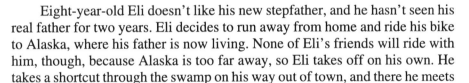

up with the Swamp Man. Is this the man everyone has been afraid of for so long? The Swamp Man just might have some information about learning to live with change. This is an important story about acceptance that will win the hearts of younger readers.

B.D.V.

Mothers

Griffin, Adele
6-8 Split Just Right

Hyperion Books for Children. 1997.   ISBN: 0-7868-2288-0. 176 p.

Dandelion—Danny for short—is a fifteen-year-old girl who was raised by her sometimes flaky actress-mother. Supposedly, her father left when she was a baby and her parents were divorced. Now Danny's mother teaches part-time at Bradshaw, a school for girls, that Danny attends without having to pay tuition. When Danny finds out that her mother is keeping secrets, she begins to wonder how much of the information her mother has given her is actually the truth. Griffin speaks directly to older readers who are in single-parent situations. It is a well-paced, believable story about the balancing act that takes place in mother/daughter families.

B.D.V.

High, Linda Oatman
Maizie

Holiday House. 1995.   ISBN: 0-8234-1161-3. 180 p.

Maizie was only eight years old, and her sister Grace was a baby, when their mother ran away. Now that she is twelve, Maizie has three wishes: that her Mama would come back to Welsh Mountain; that her Pa would quit drinking; and that she could earn enough money to buy a strawberry roan pony. In this story, a strong and patient girl learns that some of her wishes can come true.

L.W.

Kerley, Barbara; Katherine Tillotson, illus.
Songs of Papa's Island

Houghton Mifflin. 1995.   ISBN: 0-395-71548-2. 59 p.

Mama's stories always begin with, "Before you were born, we lived on an island in the middle of the ocean." Mama tells her daughter stories about what life was like on the island from the time the little girl was the size of a pea inside her mother until she was a toddler. On Papa's island, you can go snorkeling and feed fish from your hand, race hermit crabs on the beach, watch geckoes walk on the ceiling of your bedroom, and walk through a cloud of butterflies. Mama's stories are like songs, and the little girl begs for more. The reader, too, is left begging for more after reading this lyrical tale, with stunning black-and-white drawings.

Awards: ALA Notable Books for Children, 1996

L.W.

Homeless Parents

Fox, Paula
Monkey Island
Orchard. 1991.   ISBN: 0-531-05962-6. 151 p.

Eleven-year-old Clay's life collapses after he is abandoned by his unemployed father and later by his pregnant mother. Left alone in a welfare hotel with $28.00, Clay soon finds himself out on the streets, where he is befriended by two homeless men, Calvin and Buddy, and taught the tricks of urban survival. His two new adult friends soon become Clay's only family, as the three share many harrowing moments before he is finally reunited with his mother and new baby sister. A beautifully written survival story that frankly examines the traumatic lives of the homeless. A must-read.

C.P.S.

Siblings

Banks, Jacqueline Turner
Egg-Drop Blues
Houghton Mifflin. 1995.   ISBN: 0-395-70931-8. 120 p.

Judge, a twelve-year-old sixth-grader, is failing in school because of his dyslexia. If he takes part in a science competition, he can get extra points and avoid being transferred, along with his brother, to another school. The new school is known to be hostile towards African American students, and the boys would rather stay where they are accepted. Judge and his brother work together and make the best project ever for the competition. Turner shows a close-knit family with identical twins who demonstrate very different personalities. Tension and humor combine in this lively story for middle readers.

B.D.V.

Betsy Byars's books are always a treat, and this series about Bingo Brown is exactly what her fans love the most. Bingo Brown is a delightfully funny character who is finding out about life and love. He is honest and likeable and everything a person hopes to find when looking for a new friend. Every one of the books in the Bingo Brown series is just as laugh-out-loud funny as the next.

Byars, Betsy
Bingo Brown, Gypsy Lover
Viking. 1990.   ISBN: 0-670-83322-3. 122 p.

Bingo Brown felt pretty accomplished in his long-distance relationship with Melissa. She had told a friend that he reminded her of the gypsy lover, a character in the romance novel her sister was reading. His mood changes, though, when he receives a Christmas present in the mail from Melissa but has nothing for her. His parents are no help at all, because his mother is pregnant with his little brother. Does Bingo even want this new intrusion in his life? What if the baby made an early appearance and was sick or even worse? Middle readers will identify with Bingo in this heartwarming and funny story about Bingo's ongoing efforts to move into the teen years.

Series/Sequels: *Bingo Brown and the Language of Love*; *The Burning Questions of Bingo Brown*; *Bingo Brown, Gypsy Lover*; *Bingo Brown's Guide to Romance*

B.D.V.

B yars follows this tale with the last in the series that is just as funny as the other three. It will ring true for boys and girls alike as they try to figure out dating, romance and all the difficulties of the opposite sex.

Byars, Betsy
Bingo Brown's Guide to Romance

Viking. 1992.   ISBN: 0-670-844918. 115 p.

Now that Bingo Brown is in junior high, and has so much experience in life and romance (?!), he is writing a book on romance for his little brother Jamie. Jamie is still a tiny baby, but Bingo knows that Jamie will thank him for all the advice when he is older. When Melissa, Bingo's old girlfriend returns to town, Bingo has more embarrassing, bungling, and always hilarious bits of wisdom to pass on to Jamie than anything else. Bingo continues to endear himself to the readers as they laugh with him through every one of his heartwarming attempts at romance, or even engaging in conversation with the opposite sex. First time Bingo readers, and all of his already established fans, will delight in Byars' fourth book about Bingo Brown.

Series/Sequels: *Bingo Brown and the Language of Love; The Burning Questions of Bingo Brown; Bingo Brown; Gypsy Lover; Bingo Brown's Guide to Romance.*

B.D.V.

Conly, Jane Leslie
Trout Summer

Henry Holt. 1995.   ISBN: 0-8050-3933-3. 234 p.

Thirteen-year-old Shana and her twelve-year-old brother, Cody, must learn to deal with the effects of divorce and separation when their father leaves the family. They grudgingly move to the city where their mother finds work, but they all miss country life. The family then moves to a cabin by the river in rural Pennsylvania for the summer, leaving Shana and Cody with a lot of unsupervised time. They fish and explore, but eventually meet up with a strange, elderly man who acts angry toward them, but eventually gives them a different perspective on life. This bittersweet coming-of-age novel about responsibility will appeal to older readers.

Awards: ALA Notable Books for Children, 1996; ALA Best Books for Young Adults, 1996

B.D.V.

Ellis, Sarah
Out of the Blue

Margaret K. McElderry. 1995.   ISBN: 0-689-80025-8. 120 p.

Twelve-year-old Megan gets more than she bargained for on her birthday. She was hoping for an exciting trip for her family's summer vacation. Instead, Megan finds out that she has a twenty-four-year-old half-sister who will be coming to visit. Megan's mother was only seventeen and not married when she had this baby, and she chose to give the baby up for adoption. This gives the idea of having a sister a whole new meaning for Megan, and it turns the world as she knows it upside down. The subject matter is handled well in this book, which is ideal for older readers looking for material on this subject.

B.D.V.

Lowry, Lois; Diane De Groat, illus.
See You Around, Sam

Houghton Mifflin. 1996. ISBN: 0-395-81664-5. 113 p.

Four-year-old Sam Krupnik, Anastasia's little brother, is extraordinarily excited about the swap he made at preschool and is dismayed when his mother doesn't share his enthusiasm over his new plastic fangs. After Mom lays down the law about not wearing them in the house, Sam decides that his only alternative is to run away to Alaska. The humor in this third book about Sam will appeal to older children, who will probably remember with nostalgia their own thwarted attempts to leave home. The story is a fabulous read-aloud for younger children.

Series/Sequels: *See the Anastasia series, by Lois Lowry* (p. 70).

C.P.S.

McKay, Hilary
Exiles in Love

Margaret K. McElderry. 1998. ISBN: 0-689-81752-5. 170 p.

The four Conroy sisters, once again, are right in the middle of some priceless situations. Rachel has been nominated May Queen, Phoebe is going to be an international spy, and Naomi has dyed her hair purple. These things are nothing compared to the crushes that fourteen-year-old Ruth has developed on all sorts of boys and men. Big Grandma calls this the "family failure" and takes the girls to France for a week so they can rest and recuperate. It could be Big Grandma, though, who has the very worst case of the "family failure" when she meets up with an old friend in France. McKay is right on target with this delightful addition to the series. Middle readers will be giggling to the very end.

Series/Sequels: *The Exiles*; *The Exiles at Home*; *The Exiles in Love*

B.D.V.

Polacco, Patricia, au. and illus.
My Rotten Redheaded Older Brother

Simon & Schuster Books for Young Readers. 1994. ISBN: 0-671-72751-6. Unpaged.

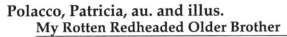

Patricia has the most obnoxious older brother, named Richard. He has ugly, orange, curly hair that looks like wire protruding from his head. He is covered with freckles, wears ridiculous glasses, and usually has a stupid-looking grin plastered on his face. He grins so much because he is better at everything that he and Patricia do. He can run faster, jump higher, spit farther, and even burp louder than Patricia. Patricia wishes on a star to do something—anything!—better than Richard, and when she finally does, she learns about a new side to her rotten older brother. Polacco's story about her own brother is both funny and heartwarming. It is an excellent read-aloud for the younger set when studying families and sibling rivalry.

B.D.V.

Yep, Laurence; Eric Valasquez, illus.
Later, Gator

Hyperion Books for Children. 1995.   ISBN: 0-7868-2083-7. 122 p.

It's Bobby's eighth birthday, and older brother Teddy decides to play a prank on him. Instead of giving him the usual boring gift of socks, Teddy buys him a baby alligator. Although "Oscar" lives only a short time, the changes that occur as a result of his short stay with this Chinese American family are both unexpected and welcome. This is a humorous, easy-to-read discussion starter about sibling rivalry that gives a peek into the culture of San Francisco's Chinatown.

C.P.S.

Grandfathers

Duffey, Betsy
Utterly Yours, Booker Jones

Viking. 1995.   ISBN: 0-670-86007-7. 116 p.

Booker Jones wants to be an author, but his plans are interrupted when his grandfather, who has broken a hip, moves in and takes over Booker's room. Booker moves to the dining room and loses both his privacy and his typewriter. His grades begin to slide at school, and even his interest in writing disappears. What can Booker say in the speech he must write for his fellow students, to convince the Middle School Board not to change the name of the school mascot, when his own life is so confused? Parts of Booker's very own novels are interspersed throughout this book, making for a funny and fast-paced read for middle readers.

B.D.V.

Griffith, Helen V.; James Stevenson, illus.
PB Grandaddy's Stars

Greenwillow Books. 1995.   ISBN: 0-688-13654-0. Unpaged.

Janetta's Grandaddy is coming for a visit to Baltimore all the way from Georgia. She has made a list of all the important things she wants to show him, but once he arrives, Janetta isn't sure that anything on the list is really important. Grandaddy likes everything she shows him, and he shows her that they both see the same stars. When he goes back to Georgia, he doesn't seem so far away. This very simple picture book, written in chapters, gives very young readers an understanding that the world isn't such a big place after all.

Awards: ALA Notable Books for Children, 1996

L.W.

Hartling, Peter. Translated from the German by Elizabeth D. Crawford
Old John

Lothrop, Lee & Shepard. 1990.   ISBN: 0-688-08734-3. 120 p.

Old John is seventy-five years old and unforgettable. He is cantankerous, independent, proud, and lovable. He is Laura and Jacob's grandfather, and after he moves in with their family, life is never the same. Each chapter title tells something of the family's life with Old John, from the territory on the corner of the sofa that becomes his. The interaction of the children, their parents, and Old John is told in a realistic and affectionate manner. The sadness as Old John's life comes to a close is heartbreaking and will certainly bring tears to any reader's eyes.

L.W.

Marino, Jan
The Mona Lisa of Salem Street

Little, Brown. 1995.   ISBN: 0-316-54614-3. 155 p.

When Nettie and John Peter's parents are killed in an accident, the children are passed from relative to relative. They are always returned to Grandma Bessie, though, because of a lack of funds. This time, the children are sent to live with their grandfather, and everything seems to be different. Right from the start, John Peter likes this grandfather. He feels that he can trust the man, and is even able to stop stuttering. Nettie likes the grandfather too, but can she believe that he will let them stay? This quiet story, about Nettie and John Peter learning the hard truths of giving and getting love, will touch the hearts of middle-grade readers.

B.D.V.

Masters, Susan Rowan
Summer Song

Clarion Books. 1995.   ISBN: 0-395-71127-4. 137 p.

Etta May's mother abandoned her when Etta May was born, and Etta May has grown up with her grandparents. Now that Manny, Etta May's grandmother, has died, and her grandfather, Gent, is sick with emphysema, Etta May's mother has returned to Liberty to care for her father. Etta May must learn to face Gent's impending death, and to overcome the hostility she feels toward her mother. Thirteen-year-old Etta May, who is a strong, spirited character faced with adult situations, learns to cope with change and loss in her life. This is a difficult but believable tale for older readers who won't shy away from a moving story.

B.D.V.

Rosselson, Leon; Marcia Sewall, illus.
Rosa and Her Singing Grandfather

Philomel. 1996.   ISBN: 0-399-22733-4. 85 p.

Rosa has spent a lot of time with her grandfather since her mother and father got divorced, and that is just the way Rosa wants it to be. Rosa and her grandfather are the best of friends. She loves the way her grandfather starts to sing whenever he gets himself caught in a difficult situation. It never fails to work, as the atmosphere changes and everyone becomes friendly toward her grandfather. These twelve heartwarming and humorous stories chronicle two friends who learn quite a bit about life and about each other through Grandfather's delightful way with a song. Younger readers will find themselves laughing right along with Rosa.

B.D.V.

Grandmothers

Bawden, Nina
Granny the Pag

Clarion Books. 1996.   ISBN: 0-395-77604-X. 184 p.

Catriona—Cat for short—has spent most of her eleven years with her grandmother, because her actor-parents couldn't take her on the road while they were working and traveling. Cat's grandmother, who is called the Pag and is no ordinary grandmother, has made life anything but boring for Cat. The Pag, a retired psychiatrist, rides a Harley-Davidson, has nine cats and four dogs, and smokes. When Cat's mother decides she wants her "darling precious" back again, Cat realizes who her real family is, and her court battle to stay with her grandmother begins. Middle readers will be swept up in this funny, sad, and always eventful story of Cat's custody battle and of her love for the Pag.

Awards: ALA Notable Books for Children, 1997

B.D.V.

Friends and Friendship

Children must not only balance relationships on the home front, they must also juggle friendships outside of the family and home life. They learn about choosing and keeping friends, about dealing with peer pressure, about making friends from different age groups and backgrounds, and even about losing the friends they have already made. This is the time for young people to test the waters and learn about the different kinds of relationships they will be taking part in the rest of their lives. It is vital information they gather for developing their own, separate personalities. Books about friendships also provide a secure, safe haven for readers, who will realize that they aren't alone in struggling to develop this personality skill—and the stories can even be hilarious!

Aamundsen, Nina Ring
Two Short and One Long

Houghton Mifflin. 1990.   ISBN: 0-395-52434-2. 103 p.

Jonas and Einar have been best friends for two years, ever since Einar moved to their town to live with his grandparents. Jonas knows little about his secretive friend, other than the fact that his parents died in a car accident. When Hewad, an Afghan refugee whom Jonas would like to get to know better, threatens their exclusive relationship, Einar begins to open up about his unhappy past. This easy-to-read title, translated from Norwegian, is an interesting, subdued look at universal themes from a European perspective.

C.P.S.

Armstrong, Jennifer
PB Chin Yu Min and the Ginger Cat

Crown. 1993.   ISBN: 0-517-58656-8. Unpaged.

Chin Yu Min, the proud and haughty wife of a Chinese official, makes her servants perform impossible and meaningless chores, just for the satisfaction of wielding power. When her husband dies and she is left penniless, the widow's arrogance prevents her from accepting the aid of sympathetic neighbors. Ginger Cat arrives to help her, not only to regain her past prosperity but also to teach her a lesson in humility and friendship. A beautifully illustrated picture book with plenty of wisdom.

Awards: ALA Notable Books for Children, 1993

C.P.S.

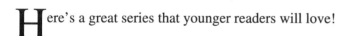

H ere's a great series that younger readers will love!

Danziger, Paula; Tony Ross, illus.
Amber Brown Goes Fourth

G. P. Putnam's Sons. 1995.   ISBN: 0-399-22849-7. 101 p.

Amber Brown is entering fourth grade this year, and she has an entire set of problems that she hasn't dealt with before. Amber's best friend, Justin, has moved away, leaving her lonely and looking for a new best friend; Amber's parents are getting divorced. As if that weren't enough, Amber's father has moved to Paris. Amber must handle all of these new situations and be a normal fourth-grader at the same time. As usual, Amber is a heartwarming, funny, and perceptive character who willingly faces each new struggle in the life of a fourth-grader. All of the books in the Amber Brown series have been popular with the younger crowd; Danziger always hits a home run for the growing audience for this series.

Series/Sequels: *Amber Brown Is Not a Crayon*; *You Can't Eat Your Chicken Pox, Amber Brown*; *Amber Brown Goes Fourth*; *Amber Brown Wants Extra Credit*; *Forever Amber Brown*; *Amber Brown Is Feeling Blue*; *Amber Brown Sees Red*

B.D.V.

Danziger, Paula; Tony Ross, illus.
Amber Brown Wants Extra Credit

G.P. Putnam's Sons, 1996.   ISBN: 0-399-22900-0. 120 p.

Amber Brown isn't doing too well in fourth grade. She's having a hard time concentrating on her work since she spends so much time thinking about her parents' divorce; and to make matters worse her mom has a new boyfriend! When things couldn't get any worse, who comes to the rescue but Max, Amber's mom's new boyfriend. Amber Brown realistically faces some difficult issues and always maintains her sense of humor in this next addition to the series.

Series/Sequels: *Amber Brown Is not a Crayon.*

B.D.V.

Danziger, Paula; Tony Ross, illus.
Forever Amber Brown

G.P. Putnam's Sons, 1996.   ISBN: 0-399-22932-9. 101 p.

If Amber Brown has learned anything yet about life, it is that no matter what, nothing ever stays the same. Just when Amber is getting used to the fact that her mom has a boyfriend named Max, he turns around and asks her mom to marry him! She just can't imagine this person being in their lives twenty-four hours a day. Amber has some tough life changes ahead of her, but she comes through with flying colors as she realistically handles these changes while maintaining a sense of humor. Three cheers to Danziger for making such an entertaining and accessible series for the younger readers.

Series/Sequels: *Amber Brown Is Not a Crayon; You Can't Eat Your Chicken Pox, Amber Brown; Amber Brown Goes Fourth; Amber Brown Wants Extra Credit; Forever Amber Brown; Amber Brown Is Feeling Blue; Amber Brown Sees Red.*

B.D.V.

Danziger, Paula; Tony Ross, illus.
Amber Brown Sees Red

G.P. Putnam's Sons, 1997.   ISBN: 0-399-22901-9. 80 p.

After resolving her school problems in the last book, now Amber's personal life has become a disaster. Her parents are acting more like children than she and her friends do, since they fight about Amber's custody all the time. It's a good thing that Max is around so that Amber Brown can know that some adults are okay. Max is her mother's new fiancée and Amber is looking forward to their wedding, if only her parents could learn how to behave. Danziger continues to tell it like it is. Her believable characters with just the right amount of humor make Amber Brown a real friend to every younger reader.

Series/Sequels: *Amber Brown Is Not a Crayon.*

B.D.V.

Danziger, Paula; Tony Ross, illus.
Amber Brown Is Feeling Blue

G.P. Putnam's Sons, 1998.   ISBN: 0-399-23179-X. 80 p.

Life is on the upswing when Max takes Amber and her mother on a trip to Walla Walla, Washington for Thanksgiving. Then, Amber's father wants her to spend the holiday with him in New York City, and she doesn't know what to do. To make matters worse, there is a new girl at school named Kelly Green, and no one has ever had a name with two colors except Amber Brown. The color blue takes over for Amber, because that is exactly how she is feeling in this episode. Younger readers will delight and commiserate as Amber Brown faces new plights and perils in fourth grade and in the world around her.

Series/Sequels: *Amber Brown Is Not a Crayon.*

B.D.V.

Fine, Anne
The Tulip Touch
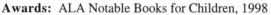
Little, Brown. 1997.   ISBN: 0-316-28325-8. 149 p.

When an opportunity to manage a magnificent old hotel presents itself, Natalie's father is elated. Natalie is lonely in her new life until she meets Tulip, a forlorn local child whose family life is barren and abusive. The two form a close, unhealthy friendship while playing mean and increasingly dangerous pranks. Natalie finally realizes that she must give up Tulip, but by doing so abandons her former friend to an increasingly unbalanced life. This is a beautifully written novel, but a harsh indictment of adults who relinquish responsibility for their children's well-being. Highly recommended.

Awards: ALA Notable Books for Children, 1998

C.P.S.

Franklin, Kristine L.
Lone Wolf
Candlewick Press. 1997.   ISBN: 1-56402-935-2. 220 p.

After the death of his sister and the separation of his parents, Perry goes to live with his father in the Minnesota woods. Because he is being homeschooled, he doesn't have any friends and spends his days alone, reading in a secret cave and tracking a wolf that he occasionally sees. His father doesn't talk much and Perry never speaks about his mother, nor opens her weekly letters. One day, the Pestalozzis, a boisterous, happy family, move into a house nearby, and Perry is drawn into their family circle. This is a well-written novel about a boy whose carefully managed self-control cracks when confronted by love and acceptance.

C.P.S.

Grove, Vicki
The Crystal Garden
Putnam. 1995.   ISBN: 0-399-21813-0. 217 p.

After her father is killed, Eliza and her mother hook up with Burl Hawkins, an aspiring country-western musician, and move to Gough Eye, Missouri. Determined to start junior high school on the right foot and join the popular crowd, Liza soon discovers that the only friend she can make is bookish Deirdre, who is more interested in science projects than in having the right haircut and clothes. Liza finally does find a way to be accepted by cliquish Amanda and her group, but soon discovers that the cost of acceptance is a price she is not willing to pay. A well-written story about a common problem.

C.P.S.

Hesse, Karen
6-8 Phoenix Rising

Puffin Books. 1994.   ISBN: 0-14-037628-3. 182 p.

Living in fear has become commonplace since the night of the Cookshire nuclear power plant accident. Now radiation is killing people and animals, and the air and food supply are in danger. Nyle and her grandmother lose their peaceful life on the farm, especially after Gran takes in two evacuees, Miriam Trent and her son Ezra. The back bedroom, where her mother and grandfather both died, once again becomes a place of illness and darkness for Nyle. Can she dare to care for someone who might be taken away? Ezra becomes her friend, but the radiation has made him very ill. Despite the serious and difficult topic, this is a story of hope and human connections for mature readers.

L.W.

High, Linda Oatman
Hound Heaven

Holiday House. 1995.   ISBN: 0-80234-1195-8. 194 p.

After her parents and baby sister die in an accident, Silver Iris Nickels moves in with Papaw on Muckwater Mountain, West Virginia. Still mourning the loss of her immediate family, Silver also regrets her grandfather's stubborn refusal to get a dog. However, Silver won't admit defeat, and takes a job in a dog kennel to earn the money necessary to realize her dream. There she forms an uneasy friendship with the owner's son, and this relationship helps Silver come to terms with her loss. This is an easy-to-read novel with a lively heroine and a happy ending.

C.P.S.

Horvath, Polly
When the Circus Came to Town

Farrar, Straus & Giroux. 1996.   ISBN: 0-374-38308-1. 138 p.

Life in Springfield is pretty boring for ten-year-old Ivy, until the Halibuts move in next door. She is excited that there is a child about her age in the family. When she finds out that Alfred Halibut is an aspiring writer like herself, she is even more excited. The Halibuts are a circus family and a little strange. Then Elmira, the Snake Lady from the circus, moves to town, followed by the seven Flying Gambinis and their mother. Ivy and Albert, who are now best friends, are horrified that there are so many anti-circus people in Springfield. Serious issues of prejudice and acceptance are embedded in this sometimes hilarious story.

L.W.

Hughes, Dean
Team Pictures

Atheneum Books for Young Readers. 1996.   ISBN: 0-689-31924-X. 155 p.

David wants to stay with his foster father, Paul, but it is very difficult for him to express his feelings to Paul or to anyone else. He continually sees the beige wall in his mind, as he has since his parents and brother were killed in a car accident. David's goal in life is to be a Major League pitcher. He is a good pitcher on his Pony League team, but he separates himself from the rest of the team and his behavior alienates him from everyone. David begins to open up to others through a friendship with his bizarre new neighbor, Lynn. This sequel to *Family Pose* can stand alone or continue Paul's story. It is also a sure hit with baseball fans.

Series/Sequels: *Family Pose; Team Pictures*

L.W.

Mahy, Margaret
The Underrunners

Viking. 1992. ISBN: 0-670-84179-X. 169 p.

Eleven-year-old Tris Catt's life has come unraveled. His impulsive mother has taken off in the family car, and his father is involved in a new relationship. Only after school, when he can join forces with Selsey Firebone, Tris's make-believe, outer-space, alien-detecting secret agent companion, is Tris completely content. Together they explore the labyrinth of tunnels, or *underrunners*, that criss-crosses the surrounding countryside. A solid, real-life friendship soon develops, though, when Tris meets Winola, an escapee from the local children's orphanage who is every bit as comfortable with fantasy as he is. A kidnapping by Winola's unbalanced father rounds out this highly readable story of friendship and change.

C.P.S.

Moore, Martha
Under the Mermaid Angel

Delacorte Press. 1995. ISBN: 0-385-32160-0. 168 p.

Thirteen-year-old Jesse leads an ordinary life as she and her family live in a trailer park in the small town of Ida, Texas. Things change for Jesse, though, when thirty-year-old Roxanne moves into the trailer next door and becomes Jesse's friend. Jesse begins to view things from a different perspective, as Roxanne shows her how to look at people from the heart rather than merely the eye. By understanding Roxanne's character traits and her eccentricities, Jesse develops a sharper awareness of others and a new appreciation of her own character. Moore's first novel is right on target for older readers as she discusses relevant coming-of-age issues.

Awards: Delacorte Press Prize for a First Young Adult Novel, 1994; ALA Notable Books for Children, 1996; ALA Best Books for Young Adults, 1996

B.D.V.

Namioka's books are always hits with younger and older readers alike. She can move easily from adventure stories to historical fiction and right back to today and still keep her readers enthralled and asking for more. Yang and her family have become favorites for readers trying to get through sometimes tense years with the rest of their families.

Namioka, Lensey; Kees de Kiefte, illus.
Yang the Third and Her Impossible Family

Little, Brown. 1995.   ISBN: 0-316-59726-0. 143 p.

Mary Yang and her family have lived in the United States for a year and still find the customs and language difficult to understand. In an attempt to win the friendship of popular Holly Hanson, Mary agrees to adopt one of Holly's kittens. She knows that a pet will not be welcome in her home, so Mary enlists the aid of Fourth Brother in keeping her pet a secret. The book describes all of the difficulties of adapting to a new life, and readers will empathize with the family's confusion. A fine, funny novel.

Series/Sequels: *Yang the Youngest and His Terrible Ear; Yang the Third and Her Impossible Family*

C.P.S.

Louis Sachar won the 1999 Newbery Medal for *Holes* because of the masterful way he has developed these rich and endearing characters in a story that can't be put down. His style is reminiscent of Dickens as every character and bit of information plays an important part in the conclusion of the story. This is a rewarding novel that will be enjoyed for years to come by young and old alike.

Sachar, Louis
Holes

Farrar, Straus and Giroux. 1998.   ISBN: 0-374-33265-7. 233 p.

Stanley has chosen to go to Camp Green Lake instead of to jail, after he was convicted (wrongfully) of stealing the shoes of the famous baseball player, Clyde Livingston. Not only would this decision change his own destiny, though, it would alter the bad luck that has been plaguing his family for four generations. This camp is actually a dried up lake where juvenile delinquents are sent to dig holes every day of their prison sentence in the hot temperatures of Texas. While surviving in this "prison" camp, Stanley finds an unlikely part of his own history, and also the person who has been buried within himself all along. Sachar's award winning novel is packed with intrigue, excitement and humor that will fill the hearts of every lucky reader.

Awards: Newbery Medal Award Book, 1999.   B.D.V.

Smith, Doris Buchanan
The Pennywhistle Tree

Putnam. 1991.   ISBN: 0-399-21840-8. 144 p.

Jonathan is a serious sixth-grader who is interested in books, music, and his close friendship with pals Craig, Alex, and Benjy. Their peaceful neighborhood and comfortable routine are shattered, though, with the arrival of the Georges, a motley, roving family with seven children. Jonathan's friends take an instant dislike to the aggressive eldest son, Sanders, but Jonathan becomes increasingly aware that beneath Sanders's rough exterior is a sensitive child worth getting to know. This is an easy-to-read novel dealing with issues of prejudice, acceptance, and peer dynamics, wrapped in a user-friendly package.

C.P.S.

Soto, Gary; Robert Casilla, illus.
Boys at Work

Delacorte Press. 1995.   ISBN: 0-385-32048-5. 134 p.

After Rudy accidentally breaks Trucha Mendoza's portable CD player, he and best friend Alex decide they'd better find the money to replace it, and fast! Trucha is one tough kid, an honest-to-badness gangster who, luckily, is currently on vacation. The best friends come up with a variety of odd jobs, and their pluck and resourcefulness make these two Mexican American ten-year-olds interesting and sympathetic characters. The author sprinkles in Spanish words, which add interest and authenticity, and the nonthreatening, large-print format will encourage younger readers to give this one a try.

Series/Sequels: *Pool Party; Boys at Work*

C.P.S.

Spinelli, Jerry
Crash

Alfred A. Knopf. 1996.   ISBN: 0-679-97957-3. 162 p.

"Crash" Coogan, the epitome of a jock and a jerk, likes nothing better than to torment Penn Webb, the nerdy Quaker boy who lives down the street. Circumstances, though, cause Crash to reassess whom and what he values. The realization that caring about others is more important than always winning enables him to make the ultimate sacrifice: losing a race so that Penn can win. Although the book is predictable, it's a funny story with strong characterization and a good point to make; give this one to reluctant readers, especially boys, who will find a lot to like in this book.

Awards: ALA Best Books for Young Adults, 1997

C.P.S.

Stevens, Diane
Liza's Blue Moon

Greenwillow Books. 1995.   ISBN: 0-688-13542-0. 186 p.

Liza is a thirteen-year-old girl in search of a personality. Her sister, Holly, certainly has personality: she's always bubbling with enthusiasm, is talkative, short, and pretty. Liza has dark hair, an olive complexion, is five feet eight inches tall, and plays trombone. She is sidetracked by her parents' constant arguing, her jealous feelings toward Holly, the distance she feels from her best friend, and her new interest in a boy at school. The characters in Stevens's novel are all rich, well developed, and often humorous. Older readers will relate to and understand this strong coming-of-age novel, in which Liza learns about life and about herself.

B.D.V.

Turner, Ann
One Brave Summer

HarperCollins Children's Books. 1995.   ISBN: 0-06-023875-5. 163 p.

Katy has already had too much upheaval in her life, with a move, a different school, and new friends. Then Katy's mother, who is an aspiring novelist, decides it would be good for both of them to spend the summer at a cottage in the mountains. Katy, who will enter fifth grade in the fall, is sure she will hate the summer, until adventuresome Lena May appears and teaches Katy many new things about life and about herself. Turner, who has written several noteworthy books for young people, once again gives her readers a strong story about growing up and finding out about life. Middle readers will identify with Katy as she adjusts to change.

B.D.V.

Vail, Rachel
Daring to Be Abigail

Orchard. 1996.   ISBN: 0-531-08867-7. 144 p.

When Abigail is sent to summer camp, she is determined to become the confident girl that she is sure her father, who has been dead several years, would want her to be. Initially drawn to Dana, one of several bunkmates in her cabin, Abigail soon realizes that the other girls will never accept her if she becomes friends with this unpopular camper. She is ultimately goaded into doing something that the "old" Abigail would never have done: pee in Dana's mouthwash. Peer pressure and the threat of unpopularity are handled very effectively. Pair this title with Barbara Park's *Buddies* for discussion groups.

C.P.S.

White, Ruth
Belle Prater's Boy

Farrar, Straus & Giroux. 1996.   ISBN: 0-374-30668-0. 196 p.

Early one morning, Woodrow's mother slips from her bed and disappears into the Virginia dawn, never to return. Woodrow, nerdy in oversized jeans held firmly by a rope tied around his middle, and with a wandering eye that never stays focused, goes to live with his grandparents because of his father's fondness for the bottle. There he forms a lasting friendship with his cousin, Gypsy, who is also mourning the loss of a parent. Readers will find much to admire in this book, especially the character of Woodrow, who despite life's trials remains generous-hearted and kind. A wise and wonderful novel.

> **Awards:** Newbery Medal Honor Book, 1997; ALA Notable Books for Children, 1997; ALA Best Books for Young Adults, 1997

C.P.S.

Willner-Pardo, Gina
Jason and the Losers

Clarion Books. 1995.   ISBN: 0-395-70160-0. 120 p.

Jason, who is in the fifth grade, must move in with his aunt and uncle and attend a new school while his parents are getting a divorce. Jason has always been a major player in sports and wants to be with all the people who feel the same way in his new school, but the meaning of friendship has changed and grown for Jason. Sports, science, and new friendships, even with girls, make this more than a story about just softball or divorce. It is a well-paced novel about a boy who deals with life in a broader way and has a great time with sports as well. Middle readers will cheer for Jason, both in his games and in the new friendships he develops, as they enjoy this fine novel dealing with many different subjects.

B.D.V.

Woodson, Jacqueline
I Hadn't Meant to Tell You This

Delacorte Press. 1994.   ISBN: 0-385-32031-0. 115 p.

Chauncey, Ohio, definitely has two sides: the black, prosperous side of town, and the poor, white side of town. Marie is a black, smart, and popular girl who isn't looking for a friend when Lena, a poor, white girl, moves into one of the shacks on the other side of town. Marie's mother died of cancer, and Lena's mother deserted her family, so both girls share the grief of losing a mother. There is something about dirty and unkempt Lena that intrigues Marie, and she is willing to cross the tight racial boundaries that divide the town to become Lena's friend. When Lena shares the terrible secret of sexual abuse by her father, Marie's secure world is changed forever, in this story of friendship and sorrow.

Awards: ALA Notable Books for Children, 1995

L.W.

Schools

School is the place where young people take on a new sense of freedom in one respect, while at the same time they find themselves guided by an entirely new set of rules and regulations in an entirely new social structure. The school years are the time when children define their own personalities and character traits in what will be their world, or society, for the next several years. These young people will be learning and exploring new avenues, "testing their wings" in new social situations, and learning to understand and to laugh at themselves in these sometimes difficult growth years. What better time to read a book and find out that they're not the only ones seeing the world through new eyes?

Avi
Nothing but the Truth: A Documentary Novel

Orchard. 1991.   ISBN: 0-53105-959-6. 177 p.

Ninth-grader Philip Malloy is a terrific candidate for the track team, but there is one hitch: to qualify for the team, an applicant must have all passing grades. Unfortunately, Philip just received a D in English from Miss Narwin, and he is convinced that she is out to get him. Philip decides to push his luck with her by humming along to the National Anthem during the morning announcements. What begins as a meaningless prank escalates into a national incident when Philip's reprimand is picked up by the national media. This is a fast-paced, thought-provoking read with a chilling conclusion. Older readers will hang on every word and have many questions for discussion when the book is finished.

Awards: Newbery Medal Honor Book, 1992

B.D.V.

Clements, Andrew; Brian Selznick, illus.
Frindle

Simon & Schuster Books for Young Readers. 1996.   ISBN: 0-689-80669-8. 105 p.

Nick has always been proud of himself for bringing new ideas to his classrooms. When he enters fifth grade with Mrs. Granger, though, things change. Not only is she strict, but she also has a love for words and thirty dictionaries in the back of her classroom. After Mrs. Granger explains how words began, Nick decides to invent a new word, just to prove a point—but then his word gains notoriety throughout the nation. Clements has created a clever, thought-provoking story for all ages. It is both a clever story for younger readers and a relevant book for older readers who are discussing censorship.

B.D.V.

The next book isn't really about school, but it is a delightful "mathematical folktale" that children would love to hear, see, and think about.

Demi, au. and illus.
PB One Grain of Rice: A Mathematical Folktale

Scholastic. 1997.   ISBN: 0-590-93998-X. Unpaged.

In a simple folktale set in India, a young girl, Rani, teaches the raji what it means to be truly wise and fair. Her plan—to ask for one grain of rice which is doubled every day for thirty days—saves the village from starvation. Exquisite miniature paintings enhance the tale while illustrating how 1 grain of rice can increase to 536,870,912 grains, in this story for readers of any age.

L.W.

Duffey, Betsy; Ellen Thompson, illus.
Hey, New Kid!

Viking. 1996.   ISBN: 0-670-86760-8. 89 p.

The Michaels family has moved to Topeka, Kansas, where Cody must attend a new school with different third-graders, all strangers. Cody comes up with the idea of giving himself a totally new, upgraded personality, a "Super Cody," to impress the other students. "Super Cody" comes from Alaska, has an FBI agent for a father, and has a pet emu instead of a dog. Somehow, the new "Super Cody" doesn't ring true for his classmates. Cody must figure out how to bring back the original Cody and be accepted by the other students. Cody is a delightful character with plenty of imagination who will be a hit with younger readers.

B.D.V.

Duffey, Betsy; Ellen Thompson, illus.
Virtual Cody

Viking. 1997.   ISBN: 0-670-87470-1. 85 p.

When Mrs. Harvey's homework assignment is to discover where one's name came from, Cody Michaels's imagination runs wild. Convinced that he was named after Buffalo Bill, at the very least, Cody is taken aback at his parents' reluctance to discuss the topic. Imagine his dismay when he discovers that his namesake was a German Shepherd and that this embarrassing secret must be revealed to his entire class! The author is a genius at writing easy-to-read novels that ring true; elementary readers will find this an easy, nonthreatening, and humorous entry to longer books of fiction.

C.P.S.

Franklin, Kristine L.
Nerd No More

Candlewick Press. 1996.   ISBN: 1-56402-674-4. 143 p.

It's hard to be cool when you are the smartest kid in the class, your nickname is Wiggie (for Ludwig), and your mother is the host of an educational science TV show. At least that's what Wiggie thinks when the kids at school hum the *Jump into Science* theme song and draw a picture of him as the class nerd. When Wiggie makes friends with Callie, a new girl in class who is just as smart as he is, things get even worse. Determined to change his image, he finally learns that it really is okay to be smart. Even "cool" guys have problems in this very funny and perceptive novel.

4

L.W.

Konigsburg, E. L.
The View from Saturday

Atheneum Books for Young Readers. 1996.   ISBN: 0-689-80993-X. 163 p.

Four very different and unique sixth-graders tell their own stories, which at first appear to be unrelated. However, the stories become interwoven as each student develops a strong and special bond with the others. Mrs. Olinski, their sixth-grade teacher, is also aware of these strong ties, and because of it chooses each of these students to represent their school in the Academic Bowl. The characters and the story develop, intertwine, and build to an exciting conclusion that will hold readers to the very last page. This masterfully developed story, which is filled with warmth and feeling, will appeal to many. It is definitely an award-winning favorite.

> **Awards:** Newbery Medal Book, 1997; ALA Notable Books for Children, 1997

B.D.V.

The Dynamite Dinah series by Claudia Mills has become a real favorite for many readers. Mills speaks directly to young people who are trying to get through all those unbelievably difficult times in middle school. Anyone who has grown up will appreciate Mills's perceptive look at life through Dinah.

Mills, Claudia
Dinah Forever

Farrar, Straus & Giroux. 1995.   ISBN: 0-374-31788-7. 134 p.

Dinah Seabrooke intends to make her mark on the seventh grade, but things don't always go her way. She isn't elected class president; she fails miserably when she tries out for the school musical; and she breaks up with her boyfriend, Nick, almost daily. She is chosen Poet of the Week, but that honor seems insignificant when she learns that in 5 billion years, the sun will run out of hydrogen and the earth will vaporize. No one will even remember she was here. Cosmic problems mesh with the everyday happenings of friendship and growing up in this fourth novel about Dynamite Dinah.

Series/Sequels: *Dynamite Dinah*; *Dinah for President*; *Dinah in Love*; *Dinah Forever*

L.W.

Morgenstern, Susie. Translated by Gill Rosner.
Secret Letters from 0 to 10

Viking. 1998.   ISBN: 0-670-88007-8. 137 p.

Ten-year-old Ernest Morlaisse hasn't done much with his life. His mother died and his father left right after Ernest was born. He has grown up with his grandmother, who took him out of a "sense of duty." Ernest wasn't sad about his life—in fact, he didn't feel much of anything—that is, until Victoria de Montardent came to school. She already knew that the two of them would marry in thirteen years, eight months, and three days, so Ernest was free to think about other things and even to ask some questions. Rosner's translation of this heartwarming story by Morgenstern (a popular French children's author) brings life to the feisty Victoria, who will be much loved by younger readers.

B.D.V.

Naylor's series about Alice McKinley is already a classic. Alice acts as a best friend to readers everywhere as she learns about her own problems. Girls especially want to read every new installment in Alice's life.

Naylor, Phyllis Reynolds
Alice in Lace

Atheneum Books for Young Readers. 1996.   ISBN: 0-689-80358-3. 139 p.

Alice finds eighth grade very interesting because she is getting married. Well, not really married, but her assignment in health class is to plan a wedding and honeymoon, rent an apartment, and buy furniture, all on a budget of $5,000. Fans of Alice McKinley will welcome back their old friend with her new problems, questions, and experiences. New readers will want to get to know Alice better.

Series/Sequels: *Agony of Alice*; *Alice in Rapture, Sort Of*; *Reluctantly Alice*; *All but Alice*; *Alice in April*; *Alice In-Between*; *Alice the Brave*; *Alice in Lace*; *Outrageously Alice*

L.W.

Alice continues to mature and find out about life in the next two Alice books. These are appropriate for older Alice fans.

Rocklin, Joanne
For Your Eyes Only!

Scholastic. 1997.   ISBN: 0-590-67447-1. 136 p.

When Mr. Moffat, the new sixth-grade teacher, wants everyone to write poetry and keep a journal, Lucy K. Keane couldn't be happier. She loves to write. However, not everyone is so thrilled, especially her archenemy, Andy Cooper. Through the poems Mr. Moffat writes on the board and the journal entries of several sixth-graders, readers learn about the students' feelings, family lives, and their growing interest in poetry.

L.W.

Scieszka, Jon; Lane Smith, illus.
Math Curse

Viking. 1995.   ISBN: 0-670-86194-4. Unpaged.

When Mrs. Fibonacci tells her class that almost everything can be thought of as a math problem, one girl finds herself trapped in a math curse. Eating, sleeping, and the entire school day are surrounded by the nightmare of hundreds of math problems. She finally finds a way to break the curse. Vivid illustrations and a very funny story make this a treat for readers of any age.

Awards: ALA Notable Books for Children, 1996

L.W.

Shalant, Phyllis
Beware of Kissing Lizard Lips

Dutton Children's Books. 1995.   ISBN: 0-525-45199-4. 183 p.

Preadolescent angst runs riotously in this story of sixth-grader Zach Moore, as he attempts to sort out his conflicting emotions regarding growing up. Zach is a likeable character whose emotional turmoil is humorously described. Although the chest jokes ("missiles") grow tedious, this is a breezy, comforting look at growing up which young readers, particularly boys, will identify with, and it has a nice, understated moral.

C.P.S.

Shreve, Susan; Gregg Thorkelson, illus.
Warts

Tambourine Books. 1996.   ISBN: 0-688-14378-4. 88 p.

Jilsy Rider can hardly wait for school to begin. However, only days before classes start, she discovers a wart on her thumb, and soon her hands are covered with them. Determined not to begin third grade unless they disappear, Jilsy, with the help of her family and a sympathetic teacher, learns that appearances are secondary to what really counts. This easy-reading chapter book will interest children who have gone through similar experiences. Despite rather unappealing illustrations, this book should find a ready audience.

C.P.S.

Voigt, Cynthia
Bad Girls

Scholastic. 1996.   ISBN: 1-590-60134-2. 304 p.

By the end of their first day at a new school, fifth-graders Mikey and Margalo recognize kindred spirits in one another: both like to make trouble and neither one cares a fig about what other people think. By the end of the novel, these two have managed to turn their classroom into a battlefield. There's no pat moral to this rollicking tale of two bad seeds gone badder, and that's where the fun lies. Despite their kid-wise teacher, they get away with every prank unscathed and unrepentant. Kids will think this book rings true and may even wonder how the author knows so much about them.

Series/Sequels: *Bad Girls*; *Bad, Badder, Baddest*

C.P.S.

Voigt brings back these two characters, one year older but full of just as many pranks in this sequel to *Bad Girls*.

Voigt, Cynthia
Bad, Badder, Baddest

Scholastic. 1997.   ISBN: 0-590-60136-9. 176 p.

Mikey and Margalo return in this sequel, and now they are in sixth grade. The girls are trying everything they can think of to stop Mikey's parents from getting a divorce. Unfortunately, they are too late even though they try their hardest. The two also make a new friend at school who gives new meaning to the word "bad." The girls learn a lot about life and about themselves in this entertaining, but sometimes bordering on contrived, sequel. Fans will pick up this one right away, while new readers will be interested in reading the first.

Series/Sequels: *Bad Girls; Bad, Badder, Baddest.*

B.D.V.

Willis, Meredith Sue
Marco's Monster

HarperCollins. 1996.   ISBN: 0-060-27195-7. 118 p.

Marco and Tyrone are looking forward to the class play, "Cool Girl and the Main Monster." Marco's problem is how to keep his hot-tempered best friend out of trouble long enough for him to star in it. Added to his worries is keeping up with Fritzi, a headstrong little sister who performs surgical operations on her dolls in anticipation of a medical career. With well-developed characters and interesting relationships, this book is a generous cut above similar material, and will find many enthusiastic readers.

Series/Sequels: *The Secret Super Powers of Marco; Marco's Monster*

C.P.S.

Woodson, Jacqueline
Maizon at Blue Hill

Delacorte Press. 1992.   ISBN: 0-395-30796-9. 131 p.

Maizon (which rhymes with *raisin*) is leaving her grandmother, her best friend, and her comfortable neighborhood because she has received an academic scholarship to the exclusive Blue Hill boarding school. Her feelings are mixed about leaving home, but she becomes even more confused at school, where she faces new questions about racism, intelligence, friendships, and family. Is Blue Hill the right school for her? Will Grandma be disappointed if Maizon doesn't succeed or wants to come back home? Will her old friends on Madison Street still remember her? This poignant but satisfying story about an exceptional girl joins *Last Summer with Maizon* to begin a thought-provoking series for older readers.

    Awards: ALA Best Books for Young Adults, 1992

Series/Sequels: *Last Summer with Maizon*; *Maizon at Blue Hill*

L.W.

Ethnic Groups

C hildren from many different backgrounds come together in books to share their similarities and differences during their formative years. Books can provide many excellent opportunities for young people to understand the unique qualities of every ethnic group, and to celebrate the richness that diversity brings to the sometimes humdrum experience of everyday living.

African Americans

Fenner, Carol
Yolonda's Genius

Margaret K. McElderry. 1995.   ISBN: 0-689-80001-0. 211 p.

    After finding drugs in the pocket of her six-year-old son's jeans, Yolonda's mother moves the family from Chicago's inner city to the quieter life of a small Michigan town. There Yolonda, a plucky, determined African American fifth-grader, has the usual problems with making friends and fitting in, while at the same time trying to convince her mother that younger brother Andrew, despite difficulties in school, is a musical genius. This is a beautifully written portrait of a strong, resourceful young girl who refuses to let circumstances wear her down. This book is highly recommended; every child should have the opportunity to meet Yolonda.

    Awards: Newbery Medal Honor Book, 1996; ALA Notable Books for Children, 1996

C.P.S.

Nelson, Vaunda Micheaux
Possibles

Putnam. 1995.   ISBN: 0-399-22823-3. 179 p.

    Mary Sheppard Lee is still mourning the loss of her beloved father to cancer. Finances have been tight and "Sheppy" has agreed to forgo her yearly summer camp to take a job as a companion to a bedridden young woman. Despite an age difference of fifteen years, Sheppy and Miss M. form a lasting friendship, which enables the young girl to come to terms with her father's death while at the same time helping her friend to find a lost love. This quiet story is an extremely moving portrait of two African American families' devotion to one another. Sheppy is a sensitive, intelligent, and strong character whom readers will be happy to get to know.

C.P.S.

Pinkney, Andrea Davis
Hold Fast to Dreams

Morrow Junior Books. 1995.   ISBN: 0-688-12832-7. 106 p.

The Jumpin' Jive Five, the double-dutch jumprope team from her neighborhood in Baltimore, and her camera are Dierdre "Camera Dee" Willis's greatest loves. When her father is promoted and the family has to move to Wexford, Connecticut, nothing is the same. Dee is the only black student in her new school. Everyone plays lacrosse, and no one has heard of double-dutch or Langston Hughes. Dee soon realizes that she isn't the only one having trouble with Wexford. Readers will admire the courage of twelve-year-old Dierdre as she and her family learn that sometimes it is hard to keep your dreams alive.

L.W.

Chinese Americans

Yep, Laurence
Thief of Hearts

HarperCollins. 1995.   ISBN: 0-06-025341-X. 208 p.

Although Stacey Palmer is the daughter of a Chinese mother and an American father, she's never thought very much about the fact that she's half Chinese. However, when she's asked to befriend Hong Ch'un, a girl who has just moved to the United States from China, circumstances make Stacey come to value her racial heritage, and also to reflect on the stupidity of bigotry. Although this book may be too long, it does provide an opportunity to learn about Chinese culture and to reflect on how culture affects attitudes.

C.P.S.

Mexican Americans

Jimenez, Francisco
The Circuit

University of New Mexico Press. 1997.   ISBN: 0-8263-1797-9. 134 p.

This brilliant collection of short stories follows a family of Mexican migrant workers as they cross *la frontera* into the United States in hopes of making a better life for themselves. Narrated by Panchito, the younger son, over the course of several years, these stories may be read alone, but the poignancy of the family's fate can best be understood when the book is read as a whole. Poverty, horrible working conditions, and the struggle to survive against overwhelming odds are described in understated prose. Readers will be moved by the plight of illegal immigrants. Highly recommended.

C.P.S.

Talbert, Marc
A Sunburned Prayer

Simon & Schuster Books for Young Readers. 1995.   ISBN: 0-689-80125-4. 180 p.

Eloy is extremely close to his grandmother, who lives with his family in a small New Mexican town. Things have been especially difficult for the family since his *abuela* was diagnosed with cancer. Eloy is convinced that if he can make the seventeen-mile pilgrimage to the Sanctuario de Chimayo to pray for her, she will recover. Along the way he is joined by a stray dog, who is not only good company but also a good protector. The extensive use of Spanish words and details about the Catholic religion add authenticity to this challenging novel for mature readers.

C.P.S.

Native Americans

Strete, Craig Kee
The World in Grandfather's Hands

Clarion Books. 1995.   ISBN: 0-395-72102-4. 135 p.

Eleven-year-old Jimmy is upset when he and his mother move from their pueblo to the city after his father's death. Even his grandfather's loving, patient help cannot erase the loneliness and alienation that Jimmy feels, surrounded as he is by unfriendly people whom he can't—or won't bother to—understand. It isn't until his mother explains the real reason behind the move that Jimmy begins to adapt to his new life and becomes willing to make a neighborhood friend. This book effectively depicts Native American culture and the difficulties an "outsider" has trying to make a place for himself in an unfamiliar world.

C.P.S.

Problem Novels

Children today must face many of life's most difficult problems at an early age. Young people deal with death and divorce within their own families, or within the families of friends, on a regular basis. They see physical and emotional problems, either with their friends and acquaintances or within themselves, and they seek out material on the subjects. They look to fiction to find other children who are dealing with these issues, so that they know they aren't alone. As these problems become more prevalent in society, it is important to have quality material available discussing these issues. The following books portray these issues in a realistic, honest way. The characters gain understanding in all of these situations, and they realize that these challenges make up different pieces in the puzzle of life that they are putting together.

Divorce

Fine, Anne
Step by Wicked Step

Little, Brown. 1996.   ISBN: 0-316-28345-2. 138 p.

On an overnight field trip to a spooky house, a group of schoolchildren who supposedly have little in common discover the hidden diary of a young Victorian boy who was tormented by an evil stepfather. Prompted by this narrative, the children are encouraged to relate stories of their own divorced families, new stepparents, and obnoxious stepsiblings. Alternately funny and poignant, these stories definitely have a message to impart, but the wit and humor of the narrative serves as a spoonful of sugar that makes this medicine go down easily. As always, Anne Fine manages to tackle a serious subject thoughtfully, yet accessibly.

C.P.S.

Honeycutt, Natalie
6-8 Ask Me Something Easy

Orchard. 1991.   ISBN: 0-531-058-948. 152 p.

The traumatic and lifelong effects of divorce are shockingly described in this first-person narrative. Seventeen-year-old Addie recounts her life from age seven, when her beloved father abandoned the family, leaving her and three sisters in the hands of an unstable, violent mother. Although older sister Dinah, as Mama's confidant, has things relatively easy, and the younger siblings (twins) have each other for support, Addie, who is most like her father, is left to suffer both emotional and eventually physical abuse from Mama. No happy endings here, yet the reader is left with the feeling that Addie, a basically sweet-natured and level-headed young woman, will survive.

Awards: ALA Best Books for Young Adults, 1991

C.P.S.

Shreve, Susan; Chris Cart, illus.
The Formerly Great Alexander Family

Tambourine Books. 1995.   ISBN: 0-688-13551-X. 91 p.

Ten-year-old Liam has always been so proud of his family. His parents are great; even his sisters are okay, for sisters; and everyone always likes to visit their home. Things fall apart for Liam, though, when his parents announce that they are getting a divorce. Liam won't tell his friends and won't visit his father in his dad's new apartment. If he can just keep pretending through the summer, he is sure that his parents will get back together again when school starts in the fall. This well-developed story shows how divorce affects the parents and every other member of the family as well. Middle readers of divorced parents will identify with this tale.

B.D.V.

Van Leeuwen, Jean
Blue Sky, Butterfly

Dial Books for Young Readers. 1996.   ISBN: 0-8037-1972-8. 125 p.

After her parents separate and her father moves out, Twig feels abandoned and unsettled. Her mother is too unhappy to keep the household running smoothly, and Twig's attempts at cooking and doing laundry end in disaster. Luckily, a visit by Grandmother Ruthie brings some much-needed order to the chaotic household, as well as the suggestion that the family plant a backyard garden. The hours spent tending the young plants help to heal Twig's unhappiness and paves the way for a reconciliation with her father. This quiet, affirming novel will be enjoyed by many.

C.P.S.

Death

Bohlmeijer, Arno
Something Very Sorry

Houghton Mifflin. 1996.   ISBN: 0-395-74679-5. 175 p.

Nine-year-old Rose is devastated when the entire family is injured in a car accident, her mother fatally. Fighting against pain as well as the trauma of realizing that her sister may never fully recover and that her family will never be the same, Rose reaches a crisis that culminates in her accusing her father of causing the accident. This book's large print and small-scale format might appeal to readers too young to fully appreciate its understated message of loss and eventual renewal; it will, perhaps, be more accessible to older, more mature readers.

C.P.S.

Brooks, Bruce
Everywhere

Harper & Row. 1990.   ISBN: 006-020-7280. 70 p.

On the day after his beloved grandfather suffers a heart attack, a grandson (the narrator of the story) meets Dooley, a ten-year-old African American who has an opinion on and answer to just about everything. Dooley convinces the bereaved boy that he can miraculously save his grandfather by performing a soul switch in which the life of an animal—in this case a turtle—is sacrificed so that an exchange of life forces can take place. The novel is alternately funny and poignant, with a genteel charm that's thoroughly captivating. Readers used to action books may find this too quiet for their taste; readers drawn to gentle stories will finish it in one sitting.

C.P.S.

Hamilton, Virginia
Cousins

Philomel. 1990. ISBN: 0-399-22164-6. 125 p.

Cammy's Gram Tut is in the home for seniors, but Cammy goes to visit her every day, even though the home is not a cheery place. Cammy loves her Grandma more than anything, certainly more than her cousin, Patty Ann. Patty Ann is too much of everything for Cammy's taste: too pretty, too smart, too talented, too rich. Cammy can ignore all of this, though, until Patty Ann comes between her and her best friend, her other cousin Elodie. Because of a swimming accident at camp, Cammy must learn to deal with death, not from Gram Tut, but from someone totally unexpected. Hamilton touches the hearts of middle-grade readers looking for help on this hot topic.

Awards: ALA Notable Books for Children, 1990

B.D.V.

Henkes, Kevin
Sun & Spoon

Greenwillow Books. 1997. ISBN: 0-688-15232-5. 135 p.

It is a hot July for ten-year-old Spoon Gilmore. His grandmother died only two months earlier, and during a humid, sleepless night, Spoon realizes that he must have something that belonged to his grandmother, so that he will never forget her. So begins Spoon's search for that special something of his grandmother's, and his realization that it takes more than an object to keep memories alive. Spoon learns about his family, his grandfather, and honesty, as he discovers the best way to remember his grandmother. Henkes's realistic, uplifting story for middle readers shows that death and memories are key parts in forming relationships with others.

Awards: ALA Notable Books for Children, 1998

B.D.V.

Hite, Sid
It's Nothing to a Mountain

Henry Holt. 1995. ISBN: 0-805-0276-96. 214 p.

When their parents die in a car accident, Lisette and her brother, Riley, move in with their grandparents in the Blue Ridge Mountains and begin the process of grieving and healing. The tranquility of her new home enables fourteen-year-old Lisette to sort out questions about the existence of God. Meanwhile, twelve-year-old Riley spends much of his free time in the mountains, where he meets Thorpe, a young runaway fleeing an abusive stepfather. The paths of these three confused children cross during a torrential downpour that traps Thorpe in a mudslide, from which he must be rescued.

Awards: ALA Best Books for Young Adults, 1995

C.P.S.

Katz, Welwyn Wilton
Out of the Dark

Margaret K. McElderry. 1996. ISBN: 0-689-80947-6. 176 p.

From the time he was a small child, Ben's mother had told him ancient Viking sagas. Ben imagined that he was Tor, a young Viking shipbuilder, as he and his mother carved wooden models of ships. After the tragic death of Ben's mother, his father moves Ben and his younger brother, Keith, to a tiny village on the northern peninsula of Newfoundland. Filled with guilt over his mother's death and rage about being forced to move, Ben finds his game of imagining he is Tor becoming more real and harder to control. Even the reader will have difficulty distinguishing between fantasy and reality in this complex novel.

L.W.

Nelson, Theresa
Earthshine
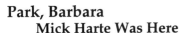

Orchard. 1994.   ISBN: 0-531-0871-74. 192 p.

Slim's loving father, Mack, is dying from AIDS. Worried that she's not handling the progression of his disease well, he convinces her to attend a church group for children of AIDS victims. There she meets Isaiah, who's trying to cope with his pregnant mother's illness. Isaiah is convinced that if they all made the journey to the Miracle Man their parents would be cured. Slim is skeptical, but gets drawn into the fantasy because of her friend's absolute faith in its validity. This is a beautifully written novel of friendship and love with a surprisingly upbeat ending. Highly recommended.

   Awards: ALA Notable Books for Children, 1995

C.P.S.

Park, Barbara
Mick Harte Was Here

Alfred A. Knopf. 1995.   ISBN: 0-679-87088-1. 89 p.

After her younger brother, Mick, dies in a bicycle accident while not wearing a helmet, thirteen-year-old Phoebe recalls some of the funny and sad events in his short life, and describes how Mick's tragic death has affected her family. Although this book is a fairly heavy-handed treatment of the importance of wearing bicycle safety gear, it's an easy-to-read, short, and at times humorous handling of a serious subject, which will appeal and, the author hopes, influence.

C.P.S.

Polikoff, Barbara Garland
Life's a Funny Proposition, Horatio

Henry Holt. 1992.   ISBN: 0-8050-1972-3. 103 p.

Horatio Tuckerman is different from most other twelve-year-olds. Who else is named after a character from Shakespeare and is a vegetarian? The worst difference is that his father died two years ago from lung cancer. Horatio is still very angry. Horatio's grandfather, a retired professor whose health is failing, moves in with Horatio and his mother. As he learns to know his grandfather, he learns more about himself and his own father. Thoughtful readers will be moved by this novel about a family's mourning.

L.W.

Russell, Barbara T.
Last Left Standing

Houghton Mifflin. 1996.   ISBN: 0-395-71037-5. 132 p.

Josh always spent his time with Toby, his big brother. Now Josh is thirteen, and the summer will be different because Toby was killed in an accident. Josh isolates himself from his family and friends and wanders through the orange groves by his house. There he meets an older woman named Mattie and her granddaughter, Bess Ann, who are friends of Toby's, know nothing of his death, and are totally unfamiliar to Josh. Josh spends the summer getting to know these two people, as he learns about himself and how to deal with the loss of his brother. Russell's novel is a tight and moving coming-of-age story for middle readers looking for a good read.

B.D.V.

Rylant, Cynthia
Missing May

Orchard. 1992.   ISBN: 0-531-05996-0. 96 p.

When Summer was six, she was rescued by Aunt May from relatives who didn't love this sweet little orphan girl. Six years later, Summer and Uncle Ob are in despair over rebuilding a life without May, who recently died. With a little coaxing from Cletus Underwood, a "certifiable lunatic" and a classmate of Summer's, the three embark on a journey to Putnam County, hoping the Reverend Miriam B. Young, a spiritualist, can contact May from beyond the grave. No description can do this flawless novel justice. It's a must-read testament to the endurance, strength, and beauty of love.

Awards: Newbery Medal, 1993; ALA Notable Books for Children, 1992

C.P.S.

Yumoto, Kazumi
The Friends

Farrar, Straus & Giroux. 1996.   ISBN: 0-374-32460-3. 170 p.

Kiyama and his friends, Kawabe and Yamashita, become fascinated with the concept of death when Yamashita's grandmother dies. The three decide to spend the summer spying on an old man who lives in the neighborhood, and "will probably drop dead soon," so they can actually witness the process of dying. What begins as morbid and selfish curiosity develops into a new level of understanding and friendship between the boys and the old man. Everyone learns more about the process of living while accepting the presence of death. Middle readers will appreciate this excellent translation that openly discusses the subject of death.

Awards: ALA Notable Books for Children, 1997; Mildred L. Batchelder Award, 1997

B.D.V.

Emotions

MacLachlan, Patricia
Baby

Delacorte Press. 1993.   ISBN: 0-385-31133-8. 132 p.

Twelve-year-old Larkin and her friend Lalo find a baby in a basket with a note that says, "This is Sophie. She is almost a year old and she is good. I cannot take care of her now, but I know she will be safe with you." Sophie stays with Larkin's family, and they can't keep themselves from loving her even though they know that someday her mother may return for her. As Sophie captures the heart of everyone on the island, she will fill the heart of the reader in a story that begs to be read aloud.

L.W.

Emotional and Physical Challenges

Fox, Paula
Radiance Descending

DK Publishing. 1997.   ISBN: 0-7894-2467-3. 101 p.

Paul's life had been very nearly perfect until his little brother, Jacob, joined the family. Jacob arrived when Paul was four and now, seven years later, when Paul is eleven, he still hasn't accepted his little brother. Jacob always gets everyone's attention because he's different, and Paul figures if he just doesn't acknowledge Jacob, he won't exist. Paul's little brother has Down Syndrome, and Paul can't accept this fact until he realizes that Jacob has his own special qualities. Fox's understanding of the difficulties that arise when there is an illness in the family is skillfully presented, in a direct and moving account that's just right for middle readers looking for support in this area.

B.D.V.

Franklin, Kristine L.
Eclipse

Candlewick Press. 1995.   ISBN: 1-56402-546-6. 158 p.

The summer between sixth and seventh grade should be the greatest time ever for Trina and her best friend Miranda, but everything starts falling apart when Trina's father loses his job. There isn't enough money. Mother is forty-eight years old and pregnant. Trina's father sleeps most of the time, but when he is awake, he is angry about everything. Compared to Miranda's storybook life, Trina's life seems dismal. This very sensitive novel, with strong female characters, explores what happens when a parent gives up hope and a child is forced to take on responsibilities beyond her years.

L.W.

Gleitzman shows that it is the character's strong sense of self, not the presence of disability, that makes a readable, rewarding story, in the next two books about Rowena.

Gleitzman, Morris
Blabber Mouth

Harcourt Brace & Company. 1995.   ISBN: 0-15-200369-X. 160 p.

Born with a birth defect that has rendered her mute, Rowena nevertheless has a lot to say. Adept at sign language, she's always chattering away with her father, an apple farmer who is the primary source of both security and acute embarrassment to this young Australian girl. Her humor, individuality, and strength are the focus of this book and readers will identify with the universality of adolescent experiences, regardless of physical circumstances.

Series/Sequels: *Blabber Mouth; Sticky Beak.*

C.P.S.

Gleitzman, Morris
Sticky Beak

Harcourt Brace & Company. 1995.   ISBN: 0152003665. 140 p.

Rowena Batts, the lively character from **Blabber Mouth** who always gives her opinion, even though she has been mute since birth, has a new set of problems that leave her feeling alone and insecure. Now that she has a new stepmother who is expecting a baby, Rowena worries that her father will forget about her. Meanwhile, Rowena rescues a cockatoo from a classmate that she suspects is abusing the bird. Rowena comes to find that the bird is a very disagreeable character, definitely not pet quality, and Gleitzman gives the readers a strong but never preachy story about love and acceptance. The story will keep the readers laughing and identifying with Rowena to the very last page. This is a good story for middle readers that can stand on its own.

Series/Sequels: *Blabber Mouth; Sticky Beak.*

B.D.V.

Richardson, Judith Benet
First Came the Owl

Henry Holt. 1996.   ISBN: 0-8050-4547-3. 160 p.

After making a trip back to Thailand, Nita's mother becomes very depressed. Nita is ten years old, very shy, and lost without her mother. One day she sees a snowy owl in dunes near their home. Somehow the owl gives her courage even after her mother is hospitalized. When Nita gets to play Snow White in the school play, she begins to blossom. Her most important dream comes true when her mother gets well enough to come to the performance. This story presents difficult problems in a child's life, but realistically depicts the good times as well, as Nita is surrounded by nature, friends, and love.

L.W.

Williams, Karen Lynn
A Real Christmas This Year

Clarion Books. 1995.   ISBN: 0-395-70117-1. 164 p.

Megan, who is twelve years old, has entered seventh grade and is looking forward to the possibility of a normal Christmas this year. She has a new best friend named Amy, and her severely handicapped brother, Kevin, has new hearing aids and glasses. Megan's hopes crumble, though, when Kevin breaks his new equipment and returns to his old, uncontrollable ways. Williams presents a well-balanced picture of the difficulties encountered in a family with a disabled child. Middle readers in this situation will understand and empathize with Megan as she learns to make and trust new friends, even though other family problems exist.

B.D.V.

Child Abuse

Coman, Carolyn
What Jamie Saw

Front Street. 1995.   ISBN: 1-886910-02-2. 126 p.

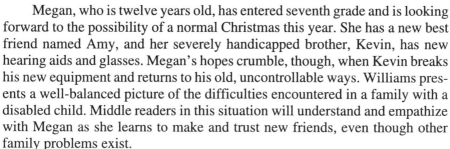

Nine-year-old Jamie was sleeping when he was awakened by a terrible sight. Van, Jamie's mother's boyfriend, was throwing Jamie's baby sister against the wall. So begins a riveting and moving story about how Jamie and his mother deal with the reality and terror that surround child abuse and domestic violence. Even though the book is small in size and the main character Jamie is only nine, its subject would be difficult for most younger readers. The story is both thought-provoking and troubling, although very well-handled, and makes rewarding reading for older children and adults who are willing to look at an uglier side of life.

Awards: Newbery Medal Honor Book, 1996; ALA Notable Books for Children, 1996

B.D.V.

Cross, Gillian
Pictures in the Dark

Holiday House. 1996.   ISBN: 0-8234-1267-9. 197 p.

Charlie takes a picture of the river at night for his assignment in the Camera Club. Just as he takes the shot, something swims across the river, leaving a V-shaped wave on the water. Could it have been an animal? Are Charlie's classmate, Jennifer, and her little brother, Peter, somehow connected to the animal? This is a telling story about two different kinds of imprisonment: an endangered animal, surrounded by urban development, and Peter, trapped in a world of abuse. Several challenging issues are discussed in this moving tale, which will appeal to older, sensitive readers who are willing to tackle the well-presented subject matter.

B.D.V.

Williams, Carol Lynch
The True Colors of Caitlynne Jackson

Delacorte Press. 1997.   ISBN: 0-385-32249-6. 168 p.

Twelve-year-old Caity Jackson and her eleven-year-old sister, Kara, stick together and try to stay out of their mother's way, to protect each other from her terrifying verbal and physical abuse. When she leaves them for good, they try to fend for themselves. Scared and hungry, they realize that they must get help. They begin riding their bicycles to their grandmother's, nearly 100 miles away. With her they begin to see what it means to have an adult love them and give them strength to face both the past and the future. This poignant story deals well with a parent's mental illness and abuse of her children.

Awards: ALA Best Books for Young Adults, 1998

L.W.

When looking for books on child abuse and neglect, be sure to see *Pinocchio's Sister*, by Jan Slepian, on page 138 in Chapter 6 on historical fiction.

Values

Children come to a time in their lives when they are faced with a real moral dilemma. They must look inside themselves, evaluate the situation, and reach a decision based on their personal strengths and courage to make the best possible choice. Reading stories about children facing similar moral dilemmas eases the way to making the most appropriate decision.

Lois Lowry, the award-winning author of two Newbery Medal books, *Number the Stars* and *The Giver* on page 108, shows her sense of humor in her Anastasia Krupnik series. Anastasia is the delightful character who has been finding herself in the most amazing and hilarious predicaments since her introduction in *Anastasia Krupnik* (1979). She also has a precocious little brother named Sam, who came into the world in 1988, and now has some stories of his own. Anastasia has rightfully earned a permanent place in the hearts of many over the years, and her fan club continues to grow with each new book by Lowry. Be sure to look for *See You Around, Sam* on page 41 in this chapter.

Lowry, Lois
Anastasia, Absolutely

Houghton Mifflin. 1995.   ISBN: 0-395-74521-7. 119 p.

After the eleventh Anastasia story, Anastasia Krupnik has become an old friend. In this novel, Anastasia faces a moral dilemma. While walking her new dog, Sleuth, to the mailbox to mail an important package for her mother, Anastasia mistakenly drops a bag of dog poop into the mailbox. She is sure she will be arrested for tampering with the mail. Should she call the post office and confess? Readers will be delighted as they see how Anastasia makes this important decision.

Series/Sequels: Anastasia series: *Anastasia Krupnik*; *Anastasia Again!*; *Anastasia at Your Service*; *Anastasia, Ask Your Analyst*; *Anastasia on Her Own*; *Anastasia Has the Answers*; *Anastasia's Chosen Career*; *All About Sam*; *Anastasia at This Address*; *Attaboy Sam*; *Anastasia, Absolutely*; *See You Around, Sam*

L.W.

Nolan, Han
6-8 Send Me Down a Miracle

Harcourt Brace. 1996.   ISBN: 0-15-200979-5. 256 p.

Fourteen-year-old Charity is thrilled when flamboyant Adrienne Dabney comes to live in Charity's sleepy Alabama town to conduct an "artistic experiment." After Adrienne has a vision involving Jesus, the entire town is thrown into a tizzy over the "miracles" that subsequently occur, and Charity is forced to reevaluate her values, relationships with friends, and feelings toward her father, the town's minister. This book is filled with humorous incidents and eccentric characters, while introducing serious topics. For mature readers.

C.P.S.

Spinelli, Jerry
Wringer

Joanna Cotler Books. 1997.   ISBN: 0-06-024913-7. 228 p.

Palmer is dreading his tenth birthday. When he is ten, he is eligible to be a wringer at the annual Pigeon Day Festival, where 5,000 pigeons are released to be shot by the the town sharpshooters. The ten-year-old boys wring the necks of the wounded pigeons, and Palmer has been terrified about this for years. What will his father and the other boys say if Palmer doesn't take part? Spinelli takes an event that happens in several places throughout the country, and shows the fear that this violence can instill in participants and onlookers alike. Congratulations to Spinelli for showing both sides of this issue. Middle and older readers will find this story riveting and unforgettable.

> **Awards:** Newbery Medal Honor Book, 1998; ALA Notable Books for Children, 1998

B.D.V.

Neighborhoods, Cities, and City Life

The places where children live have a major impact on the way they see the world and the decisions they make in their lives. Peer pressure weighs heavily on children today and, depending on the situation, children are often left to make the most logical choice available to them at the time. Here are some good books showing these children living in their own neighborhoods, whether in the United States or abroad. In these books they learn to understand the beauty, mystery, humor, and sometimes horror that exist in their own backyards. Their surroundings sometimes teach these children to make mature choices and decisions that are well beyond their years, because they have learned to understand the ways of their cities. Sometimes, the most unlikely situations and surroundings, like these young peoples' neighborhoods, can bring out the very best in each one of them.

Beake, Lesley
Song of Be

Henry Holt. 1993.   ISBN: 0-8050-2905-2. 94 p.

Be is a young Bushman teenager who is working on a farm in Namibia with her mother. Events in her life are paralleled by events in a country slowly moving toward freedom. The author's beginning note eloquently sets the historical and cultural stage for Be's story. The lives of landowners and servants intersect in human ways as the country changes and grows. Be's song is poetic and lyrical. Her character is strong and memorable.

L.W.

Bunting, Eve; David Diaz, illus.
PB Smoky Night

Harcourt Brace. 1994.   ISBN: 0-15-269954-6. Unpaged.

Daniel and his mother are looking at the horrible sights below. Everywhere people are running, screaming, breaking windows, and stealing. Daniel's mother says the people are rioting because they are so angry. "They don't care anymore what's right and what's wrong." Later, a fire breaks out in the building and everyone must leave, but Daniel's cat is missing. When his cat turns up, along with Mrs. Kims's dirty old orange cat, Daniel learns an important lesson: that cats, and people too, can get along if they just get to know one another. This picture book, along with Diaz's striking illustrations, provides excellent ideas for older children studying race relations and the Los Angeles riots.

B.D.V.

Fleischman, Paul; Judy Pedersen, illus.
Seedfolks

Joanna Cotler Books. 1997.   ISBN: 0-06-027471-9. 69 p.

A vacant lot in inner-city Cleveland becomes a neighborhood garden, uniting a group of strangers who have no other common thread. Thirteen young and old voices from all parts of the world tell their own stories of the garden during a year's time. The depth of the stories and the sheer beauty of the words will touch the hearts of readers of all ages.

L.W.

Glass, Tom; Elena Gerard, illus.
Even a Little Is Something

Linnet Books. 1997.   ISBN: 0-208-02457-3. 119 p.

Eleven-year-old Nong lives in Thailand with her older sister, Oi, and her mother. This is a collection of twenty-three short sketches about what life is like in present-day Thailand. Nong and her family live in a poorer village, but it is on the brink of modernization. Some people already have cement floors in their houses, and a water main is being installed throughout the village so people won't have to get their water from the well. All of this change is often confusing for Nong and her family, as old customs die and new practices become the norm. These vignettes paint an informative picture of life for countries involved in social change. It would be useful for middle readers studying life in Thailand.

B.D.V.

Hiçyilmaz, Gaye
Against the Storm

Little, Brown. 1992.   ISBN: 0-316-36078-3. 200 p.

Twelve-year-old Mehmet has been living happily in a small village in Turkey. Now, poverty threatens his family, and they must move to the crowded city of Ankara. The city offers even less for Mehmet's family, as there is no work and no place to live. They move to a shabby apartment, still under construction, that belongs to Mehmet's rich and unscrupulous uncle. Daily life is a struggle for survival until he befriends Muhlis, a homeless orphan who lives on the streets. Now, Mehmet must decide where his allegiances lie, in this excellent but sobering picture of street life in Turkey. Older readers will relate to the story, but be aware that there is a tragic end for one of the characters.

Awards: ALA Notable Books for Children, 1992

B.D.V.

Macaulay, David, au. and illus.
Rome Antics

Houghton Mifflin. 1997.   ISBN: 0-395-82289-3. 79 p.

A carrier pigeon with an important message bound for Rome is released in the Italian hills. As the pigeon flies, the reader enjoys an intricate visual and verbal view of both ancient and modern parts of the city of Rome. David Macaulay's drawings are filled with vitality and humor as all of Rome is seen, from its magnificent architecture to all the happenings of daily life.

L.W.

Mead, Alice
Junebug

Farrar, Straus & Giroux. 1995.   ISBN: 0-374-33964-3. 102 p.

When they are ten years old and live in the projects in the inner city, boys are pressured to join gangs, get a gun, and buy drugs. Junebug (Reeve McLain, Jr.) would rather be nine forever, but he hopes that his birthday wish will come true when he launches his collection of fifty glass bottles with notes inside. Somehow a little boy can still hope and dream, with the love of his mother and little sister, Tasha, even when life is frightening and difficult. This short book contains very powerful concepts and a picture of life that is all too familiar for many of today's children.

L.W.

Naidoo, Beverley
No Turning Back: A Novel of South Africa

HarperCollins. 1995.   ISBN: 0-06-027505-7. 189 p.

Beginning with the poem, "A Gift from God Being a Street Child," the story of twelve-year-old Sipho is told. When life becomes unbearable in his abusive home, he escapes to Johannesburg, where he has heard that gangs of children live on the streets. They ask for money and do odd jobs so that they can buy food. Surviving hunger and the bitter cold winter, and learning who can be trusted, make life very hard. In this realistic, poignant novel for mature readers, one feels the difficulties of living in a society where peace and safety are still a dream.

L.W.

Nye, Naomi Shihab
Habibi

Simon & Schuster Books for Young Readers. 1997.   ISBN: 0-689-80149-1. 259 p.

Fourteen-year-old Liyana has spent her life in St. Louis, Missouri, but now her family is moving to Jerusalem. Liyana, her brother Rafik, and her mother were all born and raised in the United States, but Liyana's father was born in Israel and is Arab. Liyana's father wants to return to his homeland, introduce his American family to his relatives, and show his family the country of his birth. Now the Abboud family must adjust not only to a new lifestyle, with a language and customs that are totally foreign to them, but also to the strained environment that exists between the Jews and the Palestinians. Older readers looking for information on this subject will be rewarded by this beautifully written story.

Awards: ALA Notable Books for Children, 1997; ALA Best Books for Young Adults, 1997

B.D.V.

Paulsen, Gary
6-8 The Monument

Delacorte Press. 1991.   ISBN: 0-385-30518-4. 151 p.

Abandoned at birth and raised in a Catholic orphanage, thirteen-year-old Rachel Ellen Turner, caramel colored and lame, estimates her chances of being adopted at zip. Her life changes abruptly when Emma and Fred Hemesvedt decide to take her and she moves to Bolton, Kansas, population 2,000. Despite living with alcoholics who are drunk by 9 A.M., Rachel realizes that her life is considerably better, particularly after she meets Python, a flea-bitten wreck of a dog, and Mick Strum, a drifter/artist who has been commissioned to design a war memorial for the town. Paulsen waxes philosophic in this departure from his adventure stories. Despite a winning female character and easygoing prose, some young readers might leave this one midstream. This is a thought-provoking story for that special, dedicated, older reader.

Awards: ALA Best Books for Young Adults, 1991

C.P.S.

Pausewang, Gudrun
6-8 Fall-Out

Viking. 1995.   ISBN: 0-670-086104-9. 172 p.

Fourteen-year-old Janna has been left alone to care for her younger brother, Uli, when an accident at the nearby nuclear power plant is announced. Realizing that the wind's direction and velocity make flight imperative, the children attempt to leave amidst an atmosphere of panic, in which common rules of civilized behavior are all but ignored. Uli's tragic death, after being hit by a fleeing car, and Janna's slow and painful recovery from the devastating effects not only of radiation but also of her parents' deaths, are haunt ingly described. Mature readers will find that this book is not soon forgotten.

C.P.S.

Rylant, Cynthia
The Van Gogh Cafe

Harcourt Brace. 1995.   ISBN: 0-15-200843-8. 53 p.

Ten-year-old Clara helps her father at their restaurant, the Van Gogh Cafe, in Flowers, Kansas. There is something magical about the café. The building used to be a theater, and maybe some of the magic from the perform- ances stayed on the walls, but something mysterious is always happening there. That is why Clara likes to be there: to see the magic come. All of the cus- tomers become aware of the possibilities around them, if they are willing to take the time to watch and wait a bit. Younger readers or a group will find themselves wondering with curiosity and delight about the magic that seems to happen in the little café in Flowers, Kansas.

Awards: ALA Notable Books for Children, 1996

B.D.V.

Schami, Rafik. Translated from the German by Rika Lesser
A Hand Full of Stars

Dutton Chldren's Books. 1990.   ISBN: 0-525-44535-8. 195 p.

A fourteen-year-old Syrian boy with aspirations of becoming a journalist begins a diary in which he recounts the joys and difficulties of life in Damas- cus. Interspersed with the universal experiences of school, puppy love, and quarrels with parents is a sobering account of growing up poor in a country fa- miliar with governmental instability and acts of terrorism. This book offers an interesting look at a little-known culture, but requires a mature reader. An aus- tere cover might discourage the faint of heart.

Awards: ALA Notable Books for Children, 1990

C.P.S.

Spinelli, Jerry
Maniac Magee

Little, Brown. 1990.   ISBN: 0-316-80722-2. 184 p.

When Jeffrey Lionel Magee's parents died in an accident, he was only three years old. When he ran away from his aunt and uncle eight years later, he literally kept on running, eventually reaching legendary status for his athletic abilities. He acquired the name "Maniac Magee" not only for his running, but also for his batting, pitching, and scoring skills in the ballpark. He broke rec- ords that had been untouchable until he came, and he broke open the way that society looked at itself. Spinelli presents both a thrilling athlete and a heart- wrenching orphan who is simply looking for a place to call home. Middle and upper readers will cheer and cry for Maniac Magee, and stay with his every move to the very last page.

Awards: Newbery Medal Book, 1991

B.D.V.

Williams, Vera B., au. and illus.
Scooter

Greenwillow Books. 1993.   ISBN: 0-688-09376-0. 150 p.

Elana Rose Rosen has just moved to Melon Hill, an apartment complex in the city. She and her mom share 8E, a one-room apartment. The action centers around Elana Rose's most prized possession, a beautiful blue and silver scooter which she rides with great skill. Through the eyes of Elana Rose Rosen, younger readers explore the sights and sounds of the city as she makes friends, especially with Petey, the little neighbor boy who has never spoken until he whispers an important message to Elana. The book is illustrated with engaging drawings, acrostics, lists, and charts, which add great interest to this easygoing story of city life.

L.W.

Wolff, Virginia Euwer
Make Lemonade

Henry Holt. 1993.   ISBN: 0-805-02228-7. 200 p.

LaVaughn and her mother's shared dream is for her to attend college, but she needs money. When this determined, level-headed fourteen-year-old sees an ad on the school bulletin board ("Babysitter Needed Bad") , she's compelled to check it out. She soon finds herself in a seemingly hopeless situation: helping out a teen mother of two who lives in chaotic, filthy conditions. Her philosophy of making the best of the hand you've been dealt inspires Jolly to get her life under control and return to school. The novel's free-verse narrative simply shines; highly recommended.

Awards: Children's Book Award, 1993.

C.P.S.

Short Stories

S everal authors are now writing collections of short stories for children. Authors are putting together stories on different subjects about the same characters, or on various characters who are going through similar experiences. The stories are often just what's needed for readers who want to find some fast reading for a school assignment, or who are looking for more stories by a favorite author, or who just have some extra time and are looking for some good, quick reading. Whatever the reason, there are lots of good collections out there, with more appearing every week, for young readers. These shouldn't be missed when you're looking for new material.

Ahlberg, Allan; Fritz Wegner, illus.
The Better Brown Stories

Viking. 1995.   ISBN: 0-670-85894-3. 96 p.

The Browns lead boring lives. Even the names of Mr. and Mrs. Brown, and Brian and Becky, all begin with the letter *B*. Their boring existence changes, though, when the Browns pay a visit to the Writer to ask him to bring excitement to their lives. Everything for the Browns is going to change. There will be new adventures, thrilling mysteries, different names, and even some time travel that will give the Browns action-packed lives, while readers get a delightfully creative story. Middle readers looking for stories with a twist will have a great time reading this engaging tale.

B.D.V.

Avi; Tracy Mitchell, illus.
What Do Fish Have to Do with Anything?: And Other Stories

Candlewick Press. 1997.   ISBN: 0-7636-0329-5. 202 p.

Avi has given his readers a thought-provoking collection of seven short stories. The major characters in the stories make both challenging and difficult decisions that act as springboards for their own self-realization and maturity. As usual, Avi's storytelling is of the highest quality, but his subject matter is aimed toward an older audience. Even though his protagonists range in grade from fifth to seventh, they are faced with such problems as peer pressure, the death of a pet, divorce, and the possible suicide of a relative. Avi's collection is highly recommended for mature readers who are looking for a good read on these life-changing subjects.

B.D.V.

Cutler, Jane; Tracey Campbell Pearson, illus.
Rats!

Farrar, Straus & Giroux. 1996.   ISBN: 0-374-36181-9. 114 p.

Cutler has given younger readers a delightful collection of short stories about Jason and Edward Fraser, the two brothers who appeared in Cutler's other book, *No Dogs Allowed*. In these wonderful stories, fourth-grader Jason and his first-grade brother, Edward, find themselves in various hilarious predicaments. Even though Jason and Edward have the typical sibling squabbles, they are ultimately great brothers and friends to each other, and entertaining members of the Fraser family. Each of the stories may be read individually, but read the entire book to enjoy all of the zany adventures of the Fraser family.

Series/Sequels: *No Dogs Allowed*; *Rats!*

B.D.V.

Hurwitz, Johanna, ed.
Birthday Surprises: Ten Great Stories to Unwrap

Morrow Junior Books. 1995.   ISBN: 0-688-13194-8. 119 p.

A boy or girl receives many birthday gifts. However, when the child opens the presents, one beautifully wrapped package is found to be empty. Johanna Hurwitz wanted to see how a variety of children's writers would approach a short story based on this premise. Some of the stories in this anthology will make you laugh; others may make you cry; all will make you think. They vary from historical or contemporary settings to fantasy. This collection provides an enjoyable read and would be an interesting and engaging read-aloud.

L.W.

Spinelli, Jerry
The Library Card

Scholastic. 1997.   ISBN: 0-590-46731-X. 148 p.

A small library card mysteriously alters the lives of four different people. The friendship of two sixth-grade boys is changed forever when one finds out about the knowledge that is available in books. The next story involves everyone at Brenda's school turning off the TV for one week, and Brenda finding a different side of life. The homeless boy in the third story is helped to accept his mother's death from an overdose by hearing a story from his childhood at the library. The final story concerns a boy who understands his life because of a new friend made on the bookmobile. Spinelli's stories are heartfelt, with a twist of the mysterious that middle readers will enjoy.

B.D.V.

Wynne-Jones, Tim
The Book of Changes

Orchard. 1995.   ISBN: 0-531-09489-8. 160 p.

Fans of the author's first book of short stories, *Some of the Kinder Planets*, will not be disappointed with this new collection of seven whimsical, magical tales. Whether describing tests miraculously postponed by winter storms or facing up to the terrors of class bullies and class projects, the author perceptively deals with the trials and triumphs, both large and small, that make up our children's lives. So well written it makes your teeth hurt!

Awards: ALA Notable Books for Children, 1996

C.P.S.

Wynne-Jones, Tim
Some of the Kinder Planets

Orchard. 1995.   ISBN: 0-531-09451-0. 130 p.

Here is a collection of nine sometimes quirky, often funny, and always endearing short stories by the excellent storyteller from Canada, Tim Wynne-Jones. His perceptive way of viewing the world gives the readers a glimpse of what could happen when certain things occur. Could Ky's house, which is a geodesic dome, be mistaken for a spaceship (with aliens) by a stranger? Will Harriet's solar system, partly held together by chewing gum, work for her class presentation? Middle readers will savor every story, as each is filled with creativity but leaves many unanswered questions to think about long after the story is finished.

Awards: Boston Globe-Horn Book Award, 1995; Parenting's Reading Magic Award, 1995

B.D.V.

Jack Gantos has written two collections of short stories for children that have received excellent reviews. Both books are filled with a tongue-in-cheek sense of humor that middle readers, especially boys, will find amusing. Pick these up if you're looking for a chuckle.

Jack's New Power: Stories from a Caribbean Year (1995)

Jack's Black Book (1997)

Paperback Contemporary Life Series

Children's paperbacks in series have become big business in the publishing industry. They have also become a source of fun and relaxation for children today. Whenever we can, we recommend the best possible books to these young readers. The primary goal, though, is to encourage children to read; to instill the reading habit in the young before they leave the elementary grades so they can see that reading is much more than just a school assignment. When all recommendations and encouragement are over, we hope that we've provided an opportunity for children to see reading as a new friend, a companion, and a source of knowledge and self-esteem.

Series: The Baby-Sitters' Club

Author: Martin, Ann M.

Publisher: Scholastic

Kristy, the president and mastermind behind the Baby-Sitters' Club, identified a need in the community of Stoneybrook: a place to find well-qualified, reliable baby-sitters for hire. Thus the BSC (Baby-Sitters' Club) was formed. The club is made up of seven official and two associate members who share all of their humorous, sometimes difficult, but always eventful lives with the readers.

Titles:
1. *Kristy's Great Idea*
2. *Claudia and the Phantom Phone Calls*
3. *The Truth about Stacey*
4. *Mary Anne Saves the Day*
5. *Dawn and the Impossible Three*
6. *Kristy's Big Day*
7. *Claudia and Mean Janine*
8. *Boy-Crazy Stacey*
9. *The Ghost at Dawn's House*
10. *Logan Likes Mary Anne!*
11. *Kristy and the Snobs*
12. *Claudia and the New Girl*
13. *Good-bye Stacey, Good-bye*
14. *Hello, Mallory*
15. *Little Miss Stoneybrook ... and Dawn*
16. *Jessi's Secret Language*
17. *Mary Anne's Bad-Luck Mystery*
18. *Stacey's Mistake*
19. *Claudia and the Bad Joke*

64. *Dawn's Family Feud*
65. *Stacey's Big Crush*
66. *Maid Mary Anne*

67. *Dawn's Big Move*
68. *Jessi and the Bad Baby-sitter*
69. *Get Well Soon, Mallory!*
70. *Stacey and the Cheerleaders*
71. *Claudia and the Perfect Boy*
72. *Dawn and the We * Kids Club*

73. *Mary Anne and Miss Priss*
74. *Kristy and the Copycat*
75. *Jessi's Horrible Prank*
76. *Stacey's Lie*
77. *Dawn and Whitney, Friends Forever*
78. *Claudia and Crazy Peaches*
79. *Mary Anne Breaks the Rules*

80. *Mallory Pike, #1 Fan*
81. *Kristy and Mr. Mom*
82. *Jessi and the Troublemaker*
83. *Stacey vs. The BSC*
84. *Dawn and the School Spirit War*
85. *Claudia Kishi, Live from WSTO!*
86. *Mary Anne and Camp BSC*

87. *Stacey and the Bad Girls*
88. *Farewell, Dawn*
89. *Kristy and the Dirty Diapers*
90. *Welcome to the BSC, Abby*
91. *Claudia and the First Thanksgiving*
92. *Mallory's Christmas Wish*

93. *Mary Anne and the Memory Garden*
94. *Stacey McGill, Super Sitter*
95. *Kristy + Bart = ?*
96. *Abby's Lucky Thirteen*
97. *Claudia and the World's Cutest Baby*
98. *Dawn and Too Many Sitters*

99. *Stacey's Broken Heart*
100. *Kristy's Worst Idea*
101. *Claudia Kishi, Middle School Dropout*
102. *Mary Anne and the Little Princess*
103. *Happy Holidays, Jessi*
104. *Abby's Twin*
105. *Stacey the Math Whiz*
106. *Claudia, Queen of the Seventh Grade*
107. *Mind Your Own Business, Kristy!*

108. *Don't Give Up, Mallory*
109. *Mary Anne to the Rescue*
110. *Abby the Bad Sport*
111. *Stacey's Secret Friend*
112. *Kristy and the Sister War*
113. *Claudia Makes Up Her Mind*
114. *The Secret Life of Mary Anne Spier*

The Baby-Sitters Club has been a tremendously popular, well-received series. Girls can identify with the club members and relate to them as they finish elementary school and move on to the fun, and the difficulties, of middle school. Readers wanting more stories about the BSC have gotten what they wanted.

Series: The Baby-Sitters Club Mysteries

Author: Martin, Ann M.

Publisher: Scholastic

Titles:
1. *Stacey and the Missing Ring*
2. *Beware, Dawn!*
3. *Mallory and the Ghost Cat*
4. *Kristy and the Missing Child*
5. *Mary Anne and the Secret in the Attic*
6. *The Mystery at Claudia's House*
7. *Dawn and the Disappearing Dogs*
8. *Jessi and the Jewel Thieves*
9. *Kristy and the Haunted Mansion*
10. *Stacey and the Mystery Money*
11. *Claudia and the Mystery at the Museum*
12. *Dawn and the Surfer Ghost*
13. *Mary Anne and the Library Monster*
14. *Stacey and the Mystery at the Mall*
15. *Kristy and the Vampires*
16. *Claudia and the Clue in the Photograph*
17. *Dawn and the Halloween Mystery*
18. *Stacey and the Mystery at the Empty House*
19. *Kristy and the Missing Fortune*
20. *Mary Anne and the Zoo Mystery*
21. *Claudia and the Recipe for Danger*
22. *Stacey and the Haunted Masquerade*
23. *Abby and the Secret Society*
24. *Mary Anne and the Silent Witness*
25. *Kristy and the Middle School Vandal*
26. *Dawn Schafer, Undercover Baby-sitter*
27. *Claudia and the Lighthouse Ghost*
28. *Abby and the Mystery Baby*

29. *Stacey and the Fashion Victim*
30. *Kristy and the Mystery Train*
31. *Mary Anne and the Music Box Secret*
32. *Claudia and the Mystery in the Painting*

Series: Super Mysteries

Author: Martin, Ann M.

Publisher: Scholastic

Titles: 1. *Baby-sitters' Haunted House*
2. *Baby-sitters Beware*
3. *Baby-sitters' Fright Night*
4. *Baby-sitters' Christmas Chiller*

Series: Super Specials

Author: Martin, Ann M.

Publisher: Scholastic

Titles: 1. *Baby-sitters on Board!*
2. *Baby-sitters' Summer Vacation*
3. *Baby-sitters' Winter Vacation*
4. *Baby-sitters' Island Adventure*
5. *California Girls!*
6. *New York, New York!*
7. *Snowbound*
8. *Baby-sitters at Shadow Lake*
9. *Starring the Baby-sitters Club!*
10. *Sea City, Here We Come!*
11. *The Baby-sitters Remember*
12. *Here Come the Bridesmaids!*
13. *Aloha, Baby-sitters!*
14. *BSC in the USA*

Series: Portrait Collection

Author: Martin, Ann M.

Publisher: Scholastic

Titles: *Stacey's Book*
Claudia's Book
Dawn's Book
Mary Anne's Book
Kristy's Book
Abby's Book

Series: Special Edition Readers' Requests

Author: Martin, Ann M.

Publisher: Scholastic

Titles: *Logan's Story*
Logan Bruno, Boy Baby-sitter
Shannon's Story

Series: Forever Angels

Author: Weyn, Suzanne

Publisher: Troll

When Katie's parents are killed in a car accident, she must leave her life as she has known it and move in with Aunt Rainie, Uncle Jeff, and Cousin Melvin in the country. It is here that Katie and her two new friends meet up with three ordinary (!) angels who change their quiet, country lives forever in this series.

Titles: *Katie's Angel*
Baby Angel
Ashley's Lost Angel
Christina's Dancing Angel
Forgotten Angel
Angel for Molly
Blossom Angel
The Golden Angel
The Snow Angel
Ashley's Love Angel

The Authors' All-Time Favorite Books about Contemporary Life

Cleary, Beverly—**The Ramona series**

Fox, Paula—**Monkey Island**

Naylor, Phyllis Reynolds—**The Alice series**

Paulsen, Gary—**Harris and Me: A Summer Remembered**

Philbrick, Rodman—**Freak the Mighty**

Rylant, Cynthia—**Missing May**

Voigt, Cynthia—**The Homecoming**

Chapter 5

Fantasy and Science Fiction

Fantasy and science fiction are two genres in children's fiction through which readers can truly escape from their everyday, humdrum existence and venture into the uncharted territory of the imagination. The places visited are initially recognizable, similar to life as we know it. Closer examination, though, reveals that things are not quite what they appear to be. The horses are actually unicorns, and the children playing in the field have turned into ravens and flown away! Time is moving at breakneck speed to the future, where humans aren't the only species in charge of the planet anymore. The readers have come into the stories and then stepped back and changed course. They have looked at the characters head-on and then taken a second glance, sideways. Here, fantasy and science fiction fans escape from today's world and move into a land where there are no boundaries. They are released into a world where anything can happen—and probably will. Whereas the fiction in the Contemporary Life chapter (Chapter 4) is built on the premises of real life and everyday occurrences, fantasy and science fiction are restricted only by the limits of the reader's imagination. If the reader can suspend disbelief long enough to let the author's world take over, then the only constraint for the reader is how fast he or she can turn the pages. This is the time when the unfamiliar becomes just what the reader is searching for, that time when the daily grind of the real world becomes a mere annoyance. If readers can just step inside and move to the back of the wardrobe, or slip down into the rabbit hole, they will encounter an entire world filled with fantastic characters and heroic stories. Kings and queens, dragons, fairies, monsters, aliens, time travel, and the supernatural are all together here, ready to stretch the imagination and to ask the question, "What if …" with readers who want to slip into new realms never seen before.

Fantasy

Animals, Dragons, Etc.

Avi; Brian Floca, illus.
Poppy

Orchard. 1995.   ISBN: 0-531-09483-9. 10 p.

Poppy has reason to be steamed. Just as her boyfriend is about to pop the question, he's eaten by Ocax, the hoot owl, and she barely escapes becoming a tasty hors d'oeuvre herself. This once-timid dormouse is tired of being a doormat to this tyrant of an owl and she vows revenge. She single-handedly embarks on a journey to find a safe home for all her mouse family and friends. Her adventures result in an exciting and entertaining story that will appeal to just about any reader, from five to fifty.

Awards: ALA Notable Books for Children, 1996; Boston Globe-Horn Book Award, 1996

C.P.S.

Susan Fletcher has given her readers a spellbinding romp through a fantastic time when dragons lived on the earth. Her trilogy about the disappearing dragons, who were becoming an endangered species, and the people who could communicate with them, captures readers and doesn't let go until they have completed all three books. Fantasy readers will love the dragons and always wonder about people who have green eyes. Here are two of the books from the exciting The Dragon Chronicles.

Fletcher, Susan
Flight of the Dragon Kyn

Atheneum Books for Young Readers. 1993.   ISBN: 0-689-31880-4. 213 p.

Eleven years after Kara was abandoned—left to die by her parents and then saved by a mother dragon—she has become a strong, healthy fifteen-year-old. Now King Orrik has summoned her to the castle because he thinks she has the power to talk to the dragons. When she arrives, though, she finds herself enmeshed in the bitter battle between King Orrik and his angry brother, Rog. Kara's life is threatened by these two feuding rulers, and it is up to the dragons to get her back to safety. Fantasy readers will be mesmerized by this second installment in The Dragon Chronicles, and anxiously await the final volume in this thrilling trilogy.

Series/Sequels: The Dragon Chronicles: *Dragon's Milk*; *Flight of the Dragon Kyn*; *Sign of the Dove*

B.D.V.

Fletcher, Susan
Sign of the Dove

Atheneum Books for Young Readers. 1996.   ISBN: 0-689-80460-1. 214 p.

Twelve-year-old Lyf is sent away from home because it is no longer safe for her to be there. The country has been taken over by the Krags, and all of the dragons have either been killed or forced to flee to the north. The Krags are looking for Kaeldra, Lyf's sister, and Lyf as well, because they both have green eyes, marking them as two of those who can speak to the dragons. What begins as an attempt to move Lyf to a safe place turns into Lyf taking thirteen baby dragons through dangerous villages, forests, and swamps, in all kinds of weather, to safety in the north. Older readers and fans of the trilogy will savor the exciting conclusion to this series.

Series/Sequels: The Dragon Chronicles: *Dragon's Milk*; *Flight of the Dragon Kyn*; *Sign of the Dove*

B.D.V.

Gray, Luli
Falcon's Egg

Houghton Mifflin. 1995.   ISBN: 0-395-711282. 144 p.

While out walking in Central Park, Falcon discovers an egg and decides to take it home to watch it hatch. Confiding in only a handful of adults, she forms Friends of Egg, a group of friends organized to keep watch over it. After many months of vigilance, no one appears too surprised when Egg turns out to be a dragon. Although Egg is adorable at first, Falcon realizes the drawbacks of dragon ownership as Egg matures. In an exhilarating scene reminiscent of Vivian Alcock's *Monster Garden*, she sets the dragon free. Pair these two gems for a lively discussion of responsibility and unselfishness.

Awards: ALA Notable Books for Children, 1996

C.P.S.

Hesse, Karen
The Music of Dolphins

Scholastic. 1996.   ISBN: 0-590-89797-7. 192 p.

Lost at sea as an infant, Mila was raised by dolphins until she was discovered and sent to live with scientists. At first, Mila is bewildered, and the book reflects her feelings by using large type and disjointed sentences. However, she is also fascinated by this new world, and as she learns to speak and becomes more comfortable with her surroundings, her narrative becomes more complex and the typeface smaller. Mila begins to realize that this new life, despite many loving adults, can never compensate for the loss of her old one, and she returns to the sea. A stunning, must-read novel.

Awards: ALA Best Books for Young Adults, 1997

C.P.S.

Hobbs, Will
Kokopelli's Flute

Simon & Schuster Books for Young Readers. 1995.   ISBN: 1-689-31974-6. 148 p.

When Tepary comes upon grave robbers at an ancient Indian burial site, he also discovers something they've left behind: a small flute. Despite misgivings about disturbing this sacred spot further, Tepary pockets this magical instrument. Later, his preliminary attempts to make music result in his transformation into a packrat. Tepary spends many anxiety-filled nights (he changes back into a boy by day) guarded from night dangers by Dusty, his dog, until he discovers the magic that will enable him to return permanently to human form. This is fantasy at its best.

C.P.S.

Young people can't get enough of the Redwall series, by Brian Jacques. His audience just keeps growing with the publication of each new volume, as readers can't wait to follow the swashbuckling antics of the brave animal citizens of Redwall Abbey. Every one of these novels is well worth the read, and will stay in readers' minds for a long time to come.

Jacques, Brian; Allan Curless, illus.
Pearls of Lutra

Philomel Books. 1996.   ISBN: 0-399-22946-9. 408 p.

The evil Ublas Mad Eyes, who has left a path of death and destruction everywhere he has gone, knows of one more item that will make his collection complete, and that is the Tears of All Oceans, the pearls of Lutra, which have been stolen. Meanwhile, back at Redwall Abbey, a young hedgehog maid named Tansy is determined to be the first to find the stupendous pearls and claim them for her own. As these two characters match wits, the story weaves and intertwines through a list of unforgettable creatures taking part in several outlandish events to solve the puzzles that are hidden in the cryptic poetry throughout the text. Although long, this tenth book in this series is fantasy at its best!

Series/Sequels: The Redwall Series: *Redwall*; *Mossflower*; *Mattimeo*; *Mariel of Redwall*; *Salamandastron*; *Martin the Warrior*; *The Bellmaker*; *Outcast of Redwall*; *The Great Redwall Feast*; *Pearls of Lutra*; *The Long Patrol*; *Marlfox*

B.D.V.

Jacques, Brian; Allen Curless, illus.
The Long Patrol

Philomel Books. 1998.   ISBN: 039923165X. 358 p.

Jacques' eleventh book in the Redwall series is better than ever, and this time a younger generation defends all that is good in Redwall Abbey. Tussock, the young hare, wants more than anything to join the Long Patrol, the band of hare warriors who police Mossflower Woods to keep Redwall Abbey safe. When the feared rat Rapscallions threaten to take over the land, it is Tussock and his friends who save the day. Jacques' storytelling is at its peak here with all the swashbuckling by both old characters and new that Redwall fans love. Middle readers will, once again, hang on to every page until the expected happy conclusion is reached and all is well at Redwall Abbey.

Series/Sequels: The Redwall Series: *Redwall*; *Mossflower*; *Mattimeo*; *Mariel of Redwall*; *Salamandastron*; *Martin the Warrior*; *The Bellmaker*; *Outcast of Redwall*; *The Great Redwall Feast*; *Pearls of Lutra*; *The Long Patrol*; *Marlfox*.

B.D.V.

Jacques, Brian; Fangorn, illus.
Marlfox

Philomel Books. 1998. ISBN: 0399233075. 386 p.

Marlfoxes, new, sneaky and more dangerous predators to ever attack Mossflower Woods, are planning on overtaking Redwall Abbey. Who should come to the rescue this time but the very youngest citizens of Redwall? When the Marlfoxes invade the land and steal the prized tapestry that belonged to the legendary Martin, the Warrior, it is the young squirrels who reach into their hearts to find the Redwall courage and strength to bring the tapestry back to their land. This is the best story yet by Brian Jacques and his fans will be thrilled by every battle that is fought by the good citizens of Redwall. Once again, this is a real page turner that holds the readers to the very last sentence!

Series/Sequels: The Redwall Series: *Redwall*; *Mossflower*; *Mattimeo*; *Mariel of Redwall*; *Salamandastron*; *Martin the Warrior*; *The Bellmaker*; *Outcast of Redwall*; *The Great Redwall Feast*; *Pearls of Lutra*; *The Long Patrol*; *Marlfox.*

B.D.V.

Diana Wynne Jones is another author who writes skillfully in two different genres. She writes excellent short stories on contemporary life and also demonstrates her talents in the world of fantasy, highlighted with humor. *Howl's Moving Castle* and its sequel, *Castle in the Air,* are two delightful books that shouldn't be missed.

Jones, Diana Wynne
Castle in the Air

Greenwillow Books. 1990. ISBN: 0-688-09686-7. 199 p.

Abdullah whiles away his time in his second-rate rug emporium, fantasizing about what life could have been like had he indeed been the long-lost son of the prince of his daydreams. Things soon take a turn for the exciting, if not the better, when he buys a dingy magic carpet and embarks on an adventure overflowing with wizards, witches, genies, and a mysterious castle floating through the air. Every child should read Diana Wynne Jones, and this sequel to *Howl's Moving Castle* is a marvelous confection of the humor, eccentric characters, and complex plot twists that typify her work. A delight!

Series/Sequels: *Howl's Moving Castle*; *Castle in the Air*

C.P.S.

Napoli, Donna Jo; Judith Byron Schachner, illus.
Jimmy, the Pickpocket of the Palace

Dutton Children's Books. 1995. ISBN: 0-525-45357-1. 166 p.

Jimmy's father, Pin, disappeared from their pond, and the whole family of frogs misses him very much. As the new leader of the frogs, it is up to Jimmy to save the pond from the evil hag. When he goes to the castle to find the magic ring, Jimmy is turned into a boy. There he meets the prince, who knows everything about frogs. As the boy changes back into a frog, he learns that the prince is really Pin, but Pin must stay a prince. This sequel to *The Prince of the Pond* is a fantasy that will delight as a stand-alone or satisfy readers who want to know more about Pin, the frog prince.

Series/Sequels: *The Prince of the Pond*; *Jimmy, the Pickpocket of the Palace*

L.W.

Pierce, Tamora
Emperor Mage
Atheneum Books for Young Readers. 1995.   ISBN: 0-689-31989-4. 255 p.

When the Emperor Mage's beloved pet birds become ill, Daine joins a diplomatic entourage travelling to Carthak in search of peace. Daine uses her "wild magic" to communicate with and cure the birds, and also struggles to thwart a plot to wage war against her people. This is the third installment in the Immortals series. Readers not familiar with the series may be lost at first, but the combination of an extraordinarily likeable hero, a terrific plot, an exotic setting, dragons, and a talking marmoset will lure fantasy enthusiasts.

Awards: ALA Best Books for Young Adults, 1996

Series/Sequels: Immortals Series: *Wild Magic*; *Wolf-Speaker*; *Emperor Mage*; *The Realm of the Gods*

C.P.S.

Pierce, Tamora
The Realm of the Gods
Atheneum. 1996.   ISBN: 0-689-31990-8. 209 p.

Although Diane and the Mage have been saved by the gods and taken into their realm where it is safe, the two feel they must return to earth and fight in the battle to save Tortall and its people. Pierce brings in the dragons, the mortals, the immortals, and all sorts of other creatures; adds equal parts of humor and romance; and creates the perfect ending for this action-packed fantasy series. Fans of the series will be delighted and totally satisfied by this conclusion.

Series/Sequels: Immortals Series: *Wild Magic*; *Wolf-Speaker*; *Emperor Mage*; *The Realm of the Gods*

B.D.V.

Seidler, Tor; Jon Agee, illus.
Mean Margaret
HarperCollins. 1997.   ISBN: 0-062-05090-7. 165 p.

Fred, a very meticulous woodchuck, decides to find himself a wife. He meets up with Phoebe, a warm and wonderful woodchuck who is the perfect match for Fred—but will there be any children in their future? Not too far from the woodchucks' home live Mr. and Mrs. Hubble, two very fat and ugly human beings, and their nine children. When the older children decide that baby number nine is just too much, they leave her in a ditch. Is it possible that Fred and Phoebe find this fat, unfriendly toddler and take her into their lives? Seidler's unlikely group of characters come together to give younger readers a thoroughly delightful story, made even livelier by Agee's illustrations. For another engaging story with animals be sure to look for *The Wainscott Weasel* in the Animals chapter.

B.D.V.

Sleator, William
Beasties

Dutton Children's Books. 1997.   ISBN: 0-525-45598-1. 198 p.

When Doug moves into an old house in the middle of the forest, he initially disregards ominous rumors about bloodthirsty Beasties living nearby. Skepticism, however, soon turns to terror when he and younger sister Collette stumble upon one of the Beasties' underground tunnels and realize that all the warnings about these large, deformed, rodent-like creatures are true. Despite his fear, Doug finds himself helping them and ultimately sacrifices one of his most precious treasures so that their race might survive. A page-turner if ever there was one; readers won't be able to put this one down!

C.P.S.

The **Enchanted Forest Chronicles** is another delightful series filled with dragons, witches, wizards, and one feisty princess. Wrede's totally ingenious presentation of the fairy-tale world will delight not only fantasy lovers, but middle readers on up looking for some slightly off center, often hilarious stories that will keep them chuckling to the very last page.

Wrede, Patricia
Dealing with Dragons

Harcourt Brace. 1990.   ISBN: 1-522-2900-0. 212 p.

When her irritatingly conventional parents threaten to ruin Princess Cimerone's life by marrying her off to a terminally boring prince, she has no recourse but to run away. Soon she finds herself the princess of the dragon Kazul, who has a fondness for cherries jubilee and a need to have his Latin scrolls cataloged. Together the two go on fabulously exciting adventures involving witches, jinns, and stone princes. This is the first in the Enchanted Forest Chronicles; fantasy enthusiasts and fence-sitters alike will fall for this inventive, hilarious send-up of fantasy conventions. A highly recommended delight, as are the three titles that follow this.

Series/Sequels: The Enchanted Forest Chronicles: *Dealing with Dragons, Searching for Dragons, Calling on Dragons, Talking to Dragons*

C.P.S.

Wrede, Patricia C.
Searching for Dragons

Jane Yolen Books. 1991   ISBN: 0-15-200898-5. 242p.

King Mendanbar discovers that parts of his enchanted forest are being destroyed, as if a fire has swept through the land and is draining out all the magic. When he seeks the help of Kazul, the dragon, he merely finds the Princess Cimorene who tells him that Kazul is missing. Mendanbar has never liked frivolous, boring princesses before, but Cimorene is different than any princess he has ever met. Luckily, these two find each other fascinating, because they must work together to find Kazul, who has been taken hostage by the wicked wizards. Wrede introduces romance to this lively fantasy, and it couldn't be happening to two more delightful and witty characters. Readers will cheer as Cimorene and Mendanbar battle snakes and giants to free Kazul. The ending of this story is just the beginning of a new life for Cimorene in the next story, *Calling on Dragons.*

Series/Sequels: The Enchanted Forest Chronicles: *Dealing with Dragons, Searching for Dragons, Calling on Dragons, Talking to Dragons*

B.D.V.

Wrede, Patricia C.
Calling on Dragons

Jane Yolen Books. 1993   ISBN: 0-15-200950. 244p.

There is trouble in the Enchanted Forest again! The evil wizards have gotten into the forest and stolen the now King Mendanbar's sword, the most powerful source for magic. It is up to Queen Cimorene, who is pregnant, and six of her friends, to find the powerful sword and save the forest from total destruction. Wrede brings in some new characters who are strange, unlikely, and laugh-out-loud funny, but they know what to do to save the forest. The story ends with a real cliffhanger. Old fans and new readers alike will delight in this sequel.

Series/Sequels: The Enchanted Forest Chronicles: *Dealing with Dragons, Searching for Dragons, Calling on Dragons, Talking to Dragons*

B.D.V.

Wrede, Patricia C.
Talking to Dragons

Jane Yolen Books. 1985; 1992   ISBN: 0-15-284247-0. 255p.

It has been sixteen years since Cimorene and her troop fought to save the Enchanted Forest. Cimorene and her son, Daystar, have been living on the edge of the forest ever since, and now it is time for Daystar to embark on a quest of his own. Daystar has never seen his father, and now it is up to him to enter the Enchanted Forest and free his father, who has been held captive in his own castle all these years. Daystar isn't sure he is up to the task, but he is helped along the way by Morwen, the witch, Kazul, the dragon king, and other companions from his mother's past. He battles all sorts of evil characters to reach his goal, and fans will be cheering him on to the very last page. Readers of the Enchanted Forest Chronicles will not be disappointed by Wrede's clever conclusion.

Series/Sequels: The Enchanted Forest Chronicles: *Dealing with Dragons, Searching for Dragons, Calling on Dragons, Talking to Dragons*

B.D.V.

Elves, Fairies, Ghosts, Witches, and Wizards

Fleischman, Sid; Peter Sis, illus.
The Midnight Horse

Greenwillow Books. 1990.   ISBN: 0-688-09441-4. 84 p.

Touch, a penniless young orphan, is riding by coach on his way to live with his uncle, Judge Henry Wigglesworth. Unbeknownst to Touch, his uncle is wretched and unscrupulous and spends his time cheating others. His main goals are to deprive Touch of his inheritance and steal a family inn away from a young woman. The dire situation is saved by the ghost of the Great Chaffalo, a magician who was famous for changing straw into horses, who provides Touch with a mighty stallion to help him halt his uncle's evil. The story combines the elements of mystery, suspense, humor, and rollicking good fun in a package that will enthrall a wide range of readers.

L.W.

Hendry, Frances Mary
Quest for a Maid

Farrar, Straus & Giroux. 1990.   ISBN: 0-374-36162-2. 273 p.

Meg's older sister, Inge, is a witch with ambitions that can never be satisfied in the small Scottish town where they live. Inge ruthlessly kills King Alexander in exchange for a place in court, thus clearing the way for wicked Lady Marjory de Brus and her son to claim the throne. The only person standing in their way is the rightful heir, an eight-year-old Norwegian princess. Meg, with the aid of two friends, risks everything to save this Maid of Norway, in a powerfully written, thrilling adventure story. Give this one to motivated lovers of fantasy and historical fiction. It should also satisfy admirers of Monica Furlong's *Wise Child* who are looking for something similar to read.

C.P.S.

Howarth, Lesley
The Pits

Candlewick Press. 1996.   ISBN: 1-56402-903-4. 220 p.

The ghost of a prehistoric adolescent, Broddy Brodson, spins a hilarious yarn of how the recently discovered remains of a Stone Age boy came to be there. Aiming to dispel all of the myths surrounding life in 7650 B.C., Broddy tells it "like it was" as he describes the conflict between two rival gangs, the Axes and the Pits, as they vied for the same turf. It will require a sophisticated reader to appreciate this novel; those who stick with it will enjoy one of the most inventive plots in recent years, which is astonishingly well written. Highly recommended.

C.P.S.

Jones, Diana Wynne
The Time of the Ghost

Greenwillow Books. 1996.   ISBN: 0-688-14598-1. 248 p.

The confused spirit of Sally Melford works across time to solve the riddle of who and why she is, and eventually joins with her sisters to defeat the ancient and evil pagan goddess, Monigan. This novel, combining fantasy, comedy, a touch of black magic, and a cast of initially unsympathetic characters is challenging, original, and very entertaining. Sophisticated readers who are patient enough to share Sally's confusion about her plight will love it; others will scratch their heads and give up long before the book can work its magic spell. Jones demands a great deal from her readers, but she never disappoints.

C.P.S.

Kraan, Hanna; Annemarie van Haeringen, illus.
The Wicked Witch Is at It Again

Front Street. 1997.   ISBN: 1-886-91018-9. 123 p.

The witch is wicked in name only in this collection of gentle stories about a mischievous sorcerer and her friends Hare, Hedgehog, and Owl. Always plotting to cause mayhem with one magic potion or another, Witch is frequently foiled in her attempts by circumstances. Young readers ready to tackle longer books might well enjoy the antics of this wanna-be baddie, although her benevolence might disappoint those in search of a really scary book. An old-fashioned, reassuring novel which could easily fill many happy bedtime story hours.

C.P.S.

Matas, Carol, and Perry Nodleman
Of Two Minds

Simon & Schuster Books for Young Readers. 1995.   ISBN: 0-689-80138-6. 200 p.

Princess Lenora has the ability to make what she imagines real. When her parents try to force her to marry Coren, Prince of Andilla, she tries to escape and finds herself trapped in a world ruled by Hevak, a fierce tyrant. This fantasy is filled with adventure in worlds with invisible little people, trolls, fairies, and elves. The book provides a great read in a shorter, less complex fantasy.

L.W.

Mayne has written two clever tales about Hob, a likeable spirit who travels around London, moving in with various lucky families. It is Hob's job to watch over these families and help to keep everything in their lives in order. Younger and middle readers will delight in these creative stories.

Mayne, William; Norman Messenger, illus.
Hob and the Goblins

Dorling Kindersley. 1994.   ISBN: 1564587134. 140 p.

Hob, the friendly London house spirit, has found a new family to take care of. He is bouncing about, establishing his common routines of tidying away abandoned things, banishing small troubles, and charming everything in the household to run smoothly. Suddenly he realizes that his job is much bigger than just caring for the family and the house. He encounters dwarves, witches, goblins, gremlins, and a quest to find a hidden crock of gold. Hob tells his fanciful story, for younger readers, in the first person. The writing is enhanced by the spriteful Hobgoblin alphabet illustrations.

Series/Sequels: *Hob and the Goblins; Hob and the Peddler*

L.W.

Mayne, William
Hob and the Peddler

DK Publishing. 1997.   ISBN: 0-7894-2462-2. 128 p.

Hob, the friendly house spirit from *Hob and the Goblins* who takes up residence with various families so that he can watch over them, is looking for a new family. He meets up with a peddler and thinks that this may be his new home, only to find that he has been sold to a family on the peddler's route. The new family just might work, as they do have children who need some watching. There is a strange pond on the farm, though, where the water never moves and birds and fish never visit. This pond may not be what it appears, and Hob must do battle with the biggest threat ever to the family. This whimsical tale stretches the imagination for special middle readers who are willing to take the time to understand this subtle humor.

Series/Sequels: *Hob and the Goblins; Hob and the Peddler*

B.D.V.

McGraw, Eloise
The Moorchild

Simon & Schuster Books for Young Readers. 1996.   ISBN: 0-689-80654-X. 242 p.

Even as an infant, Saaski looked and acted different. She is, in fact, an elf-child and a changeling, rejected by her elf family for lacking certain powers, and switched in infancy for a human baby whom the elves can use as a slave. Saaski is determined to repair the wrong done by the elves, while at the same time find a comfortable haven for herself. Length and vocabulary result in a challenging novel, but motivated fantasy readers will find this book emotionally satisfying, exciting, and memorable.

> **Awards:** *Newbery Medal Honor Book, 1997; ALA Notable Books for Children, 1997; Boston Globe-Horn Book Award Honor Book, 1996*

C.P.S.

McKay, Hilary
The Amber Cat

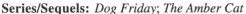

Margaret K. McElderry. 1997.   ISBN: 0-689-81360-0. 134 p.

Robin Brogan, his best friend Dan, and their neighbor Sun Dance are all recovering from the chicken pox at Porridge Hall. The chicken pox club becomes intrigued with Mrs. Brogan's stories of when she and her friends, Charley and Nick, played on the beach across from Porridge Hall with a strange little girl, Harriet, who would appear and disappear. When Sun Dance begins meeting an odd little girl named Harriet on the beach, stories of the two generations become intertwined in this humorous, intriguing story featuring the charming characters from *Dog Friday*. Be sure to read *Dog Friday* on page 23 in Chapter 3 on animals.

Series/Sequels: *Dog Friday; The Amber Cat*

L.W.

Nodelman, Perry
The Same Place but Different

Simon & Schuster Books for Young Readers. 1995.   ISBN: 0-671-89839-6. 181 p.

Johnny Nesbitt is introduced to the Strangers, the fairies, when he finds out that his baby sister, Andrea, has been replaced with a changeling. To find his sister and bring her home safely, Johnny must confront Sky Yelpers, flying dogs with human heads; the evil Hunter; a hollow man; and the queen of the fairies, who wants to keep Andrea as her own. While performing all the required feats, Johnny must continue his life as a normal middle-schooler in Winnipeg, Manitoba. This story is a whimsical combination of humor, adventure, and fantasy in a contemporary setting.

L.W.

Owen, Gareth
Rosie No-Name and the Forest of Forgetting

Holiday House. 1996.   ISBN: 0-8234-1266-0. 109 p.

Rosie Oliver likes the scary books her father used to write much better than the new ones he now writes about the lives of boring people. While her father is interviewing someone, Rosie climbs an old burned-out staircase, trying to save a kitten. After she falls, she can see her father crying, but no one can see her. She follows a mysterious girl into a forest and gets caught in time with a young boy, Alistair. They are in a fight to save their lives from the evil sisters, Sybella and Grimoulde. This story of witches, black ponds, and a literal fight back from the fingers of death is sure to give the bravest reader shivers of fright.

L.W.

Here is the series that is taking both the young and old by storm on both sides of the Atlantic. Everyone should read this series that is already claiming a spot next to the fantasy classics, the Chronicles of Narnia and the Time Series.

Rowling, J. K.
Harry Potter and the Sorcerer's Stone

Arthur A. Levine Books. 1997.   ISBN: 0-590-35340-3. 309p.

Harry Potter's life is riddled with abuse and neglect while growing up with the Dursleys, his only living relatives. That is, until his eleventh birthday, when his true identity is revealed and his real life is about to begin. Harry is whisked away from the Dursley household to begin his studies at Hogwarts School of Witchcraft and Wizardry. Harry and his newfound friends find out what really happened to his parents, and discover Harry's true destiny: to do battle against the sorcerer known only as "You Know Who," because even his name is too scary to mention. Rowling has promised her readers six more fantastic Harry Potter adventures that will thrill middle readers all the way up to adults!

Series/Sequels: *Harry Potter and the Sorcerer's Stone; Harry Potter and the Chamber of Secrets; Harry Potter and the Prisoner of Azkaban*

B.D.V.

Magical and Mystical

Lloyd Alexander's worlds are always filled with enchanting characters, whether human or animal. The next two books by Alexander are among the best of his fantasies. If readers are taken into his delightful world of fantasy, they would also be fascinated by his older series, the Chronicles of Prydain and the Westmark Trilogy.

Alexander, Lloyd
The Arkadians

Dutton Children's Books. 1995.   ISBN: 0-525-45415-2. 272 p.

Lucian, a bean counter who keeps track of finances for the king, must escape from the castle, or stay and be put to death because he has witnessed the wrongdoing of a pair of evil soothsayers. Lucian meets up with several unlikely characters who join him in his escape. He befriends Joy-in-the-Dance, a feisty but intriguing girl with magical powers; a talking donkey; an exiled king; and others. Once again, Alexander gives his readers a fascinating tale that includes a riotous romp through a fantasy land with a set of very strange, yet truly endearing characters. The pages fly by for readers looking for a good fantasy.

Awards: ALA Notable Books for Children, 1996

B.D.V.

Alexander, Lloyd
The Iron Ring

Dutton Children's Books. 1997.   ISBN: 0-525-45597-3. 283 p.

Young King Tamar of Sundari wakes in the night to the sound of travelers. When he goes to meet the guests, he finds Jaya, the king of the far-off land of Mahapura. To pass the evening, Jaya suggests a game of chance with dice, and eventually Tamar loses the rights to his own life to Jaya. Here begins the trek of Tamar's life, as he travels to Mahapura to deliver what has been pledged to King Jaya. Alexander has given older readers and fans of fantasy a breathtaking adventure of epic proportions, possibly his best ever. Readers will long remember Tamar and his quest for honor in this eloquent tale of high adventure. It is highly recommended to all readers, fantasy fans or not.

Awards: ALA Notable Books for Children, 1998; ALA Best Books for Young Adults, 1998

B.D.V.

Billingsley, Franny
Well Wished

Jean Karl. 1997.   ISBN: 0-689-81210-8. 170 p.

The small town of Bishop Mayne is being held hostage by a malevolent wishing well that is bent on twisting even the most innocent wish into something evil. The latest victims are the village children, who have all—with one exception—vanished. That one exception is Nuria, who, along with her grandfather, manages to make matters even worse with ill-worded wishes. How Nuria is able to reverse the effect of the well's grip upon her community will keep readers turning the pages of this spooky fantasy. A fine first novel by a promising new author.

C.P.S.

Cooper, Louise; John Collier, illus.
The Sleep of Stone

Atheneum. 1991.   ISBN: 0-689-31572-4. 138 p.

Ghysla was the last living member of the Old Folk. She had come to accept the new race that inhabited the earth, the human race, but she never became one of them. Ghysla was a shape-shifter. She moved through the world in ordinary shapes so that she could remain in hiding. This all changed, though, the day she saw the man she would love forever, Prince Anyr. Ghysla wanted the prince all to herself, but when she turned Anyr's betrothed to stone and assumed the woman's shape, she used the most powerful and deadly magic of the Old Folk. Cooper presents a moving story for older readers, not only about love, but also about understanding and self-acceptance, with just the right amount of magic.

Awards: ALA Best Books for Young Adults, 1992

B.D.V.

Newbery Medal-winning novelist, Susan Cooper, who has demonstrated her skill in bringing other worlds to life, steps into the world of magic again with her next two books. Cooper introduces a mischievous, invisible spirit who loves a good laugh. Any reader will delight in the magic found with the Boggart.

Cooper, Susan
The Boggart

Margaret K. McElderry. 1993.   ISBN: 0-689-50576-0. 196 p.

The Boggart, an invisible, ancient, mischievous spirit, has lived in Castle Keep for centuries. When the last Scottish owner dies and leaves the castle to the Volnik family, intriguing events occur as new technology meets old magic. The Boggart is inadvertently shipped to Toronto when the Volnik family goes back home from the castle. This absolutely delightful story with a mix of magic and thrills is one readers won't be able to put down.

Series/Sequels: *The Boggart; The Boggart and the Monster*

L.W.

Cooper, Susan
The Boggart and the Monster

Margaret K. McElderry. 1997.   ISBN: 0-689-81330-9. 185 p.

When Mr. Maconochie buys Castle Keep, he soon learns about the other resident in the castle: the Boggart. The Boggart, who is invisible and delights in playing tricks, has lived in the castle for many centuries. When the Boggart goes on a camping trip to Loch Ness with Jessup and Emily Volnik and Mr. Maconochie, he rediscovers his long-lost cousin, Nessie. Nessie has forgotten how to change shapes and remains in the prehistoric-monster form he took long ago. In this delightful sequel to *The Boggart*, readers will relish the story of how the Boggart sets out to save his cousin Nessie.

Series/Sequels: *The Boggart; The Boggart and the Monster*

L.W.

Ibbotson, Eva; Sue Porter, illus.
The Secret of Platform 13

Dutton Children's Books. 1998.   ISBN: 0-525-45929-4. 231 p.

There is a special world that is hidden behind some posters in an old, deserted subway stop. The stop is known as Platform 13, and every nine years a door is opened so that the creatures from both worlds can move back and forth. The special world is a land of beauty and enchantment, a much nicer place than the ordinary world, but the nannies from that land decide to take the baby prince on an adventure. When the baby is stolen in the real world and the door to the kingdom closes, everyone must wait nine years until the prince can return. What a chuckler this turns out to be when an old wizard, an invisible ogre, and a young hag are sent to bring back the nine-year-old prince. Middle readers will delight in this fanciful tale.

B.D.V.

Margaret Mahy writes engaging stories in several different genres, for younger and older readers alike. Here are three of her books that take place in the world of fantasy. The stories range from hilarious to whimsical to downright scary so that all the different age levels in her audience can find the perfect book for themselves.

Mahy, Margaret; Patricia MacCarthy, illus.
The Five Sisters

Viking. 1996.   ISBN: 0-670-87042-0. 79 p.

During a hot summer day, Sally's Nana cuts out five paper dolls, all holding hands, for Sally to color. Sally colors the first doll to look very adventurous. She names this doll Alpha, and then takes a break from her coloring to have some lemonade. When Sally returns, the paper dolls have disappeared! So begins the humorous tale about five paper dolls, each with a unique personality, who come to life as each one is drawn. The sisters are forever changing as they meet up with different people and move from place to place over time. It is a delightful read-aloud for a younger group, and will tickle the imagination of a single reader.

B.D.V.

Mahy, Margaret
6-8 The Other Side of Silence

Viking. 1995.   ISBN: 0-670-86455-2. 170 p.

Hero Rapper leads two lives: her "real" life as a mute twelve-year-old who has voluntarily given up speech in order to feel special before her brilliant, argumentative family; and her "true," magical life among the trees and birds of a nearby forest. These two lives become dangerously intertwined when Hero takes a job with Miranda Credence, the owner of the woods and herself a victim of dual lives, and uncovers the horrifying secret kept hidden from the world by her employer. This is a complex, astonishing novel which will be of greatest interest to thoughtful, motivated, and mature readers.

C.P.S.

Mahy, Margaret
Tingleberries, Tuckertubs and Telephones: A Tale of Love and Ice-Cream

Viking. 1995.   ISBN: 0-670-86331-9. 96 p.

Saracen Hobday is a very shy orphan who lives with his grandmother on a se-
cluded island. When Granny, who was once a detective, comes out of retirement to
capture the wicked pirate chief, Grudge-Gallows, Saracen begins having adventures of
his own. With its zany plot involving the exotic new fruit called tingleberries; a solid
gold and diamond telephone; a ruthless pirate; and a young boy who saves the day, this
clever, hilariously illustrated little book is sure to amuse and delight younger readers.

L.W.

Nix, Garth
Sabriel

HarperCollins. 1995.   ISBN: 0-06-027322-4. 292 p.

Sabriel's life outside the walls of the Old Kingdom seems almost normal. She is a
student at Wyverley College, but in addition to normal studies of Music, Mathematics,
English, Science, and Etiquette, she also excels in Magic. Sabriel is the daughter of the
necromancer, Mage Abhorsen. When he goes missing, Sabriel must cross back into the
Old Kingdom with Mogget, a feline who also poses as the spirit Touchstone, and a
young Charter Mage. The three travel toward a battle that will pit them against the
forces of life and death in this very intricate, difficult work of fantasy.

> **Awards:** ALA Notable Books for Children, 1997; ALA Best Books for Young Adults,
> 1997

L.W.

The next trilogy by Philip Pullman deserves every award and all the praise it has re-
ceived so far. It will truly be a classic, read by several generations to come, and all of
Pullman's fans are anxiously awaiting the final volume in the exciting trilogy, His Dark
Materials.

Pullman, Philip
The Golden Compass

Alfred A. Knopf. 1995.   ISBN: 0-679-87924-2. 399 p.

Lyra has spent the first ten years of her life at Jordan College, learning a bit from
the Scholars, but mostly playing with Pantalaimon, her shape-shifting but always connected demon, and the servants' children. Lyra's life changes in every way, though,
when she leaves the college and travels north to find the disappearing children, and to
stop the horrible experiments that are being performed on them. Pullman has created a
rich and powerful epic fantasy whose characters come to life. The book is long, but
definitely worth every page, for older readers in search of an unforgettable fantasy. It is
the first book in Pullman's riveting His Dark Materials Trilogy.

> **Awards:** ALA Notable Books for Children, 1997; ALA Best Books for Young Adults,
> 1997

Series/Sequels: Dark Materials Trilogy: *The Golden Compass*; *The Subtle Knife*

B.D.V.

Pullman, Philip
The Subtle Knife

Alfred A. Knopf. 1997.   ISBN: 0-679-87925-0. 326 p.

The second book in Pullman's unforgettable trilogy opens in present-day Oxford. Twelve-year-old Will Payne is desperately searching for a safe place to keep his mother while he hides from the police. He is wanted for murder—a murder he didn't commit—and he must escape. When he finds a bizarre window in the landscape and passes through, he meets up with Lyra from *The Golden Compass*. Three different worlds collide as Will and Lyra look for Will's father and the bridge between the worlds. Pullman's second book in the trilogy is every bit as exciting (maybe more?) as the first. Once again, the book is long, but the pages fly by as older fantasy readers get more involved in this exceptional trilogy.

      Awards: ALA Best Books for Young Adults, 1997

Series/Sequels: Dark Materials Trilogy: *The Golden Compass*; *The Subtle Knife*

B.D.V.

Rogasky, Barbara; Trina Schart Hyman, illus.
The Golem: A Version

Holiday House. 1996.   ISBN: 0-8234-0964-3. 96 p.

It is Prague in the 1500s, and Judah Loew is the chief rabbi over all the Jews who live in the city. Even though Rabbi Loew is powerful, he can only do so much for the Jews in Prague, and they are often treated poorly by the other people who live there. Rabbi Loew is also a kind and gentle man, so he decides to create a Golem, a strong, giant creature who looks human but is made of clay, who will help the rabbi watch over his people. Rogasky has given her readers a suspenseful and dramatic retelling of this old Jewish tale. Together with Hyman's rich illustrations, it is a first-rate choice for a read-aloud and classroom discussion for middle readers.

B.D.V.

Smith, Sherwood
6-8 Wren's War

Jane Yolen Books. 1995.   ISBN: 0-15-200977-9. 210 p.

Wren and her friends, Princess Teressa, Prince Connor, and Tyron the Magician, are thrown into the battle of their lives when King Andreus wages war against Meldrith. These brave young people join forces in the battle, using their finely honed skills of magic, shape-shifting, and that special ability of communicating through scrying. But will this be enough to overcome the terrible magic of King Andreus? Sherwood has given his readers another exciting adventure in his newest book in the series about Wren. Older readers will delight in reading more about these crafty characters.

Series/Sequels: *Wren to the Rescue*; *Wren's Quest*; *Wren's War*

B.D.V.

Van Allsburg, Chris
[6-8] The Sweetest Fig

Houghton Mifflin. 1993.   ISBN: 0-395-67346-1. Unpaged.

A sadistic dentist gets his comeuppance in this superbly illustrated picture book for older children. Monsieur Bibot, a hideously fastidious and mercenary French gentleman, lives alone save for his ill-treated dog, Marcel. One day a poor woman gives him two magic figs in lieu of payment for dental services, insisting that they will literally make his dreams come true. The first does, in totally unexpected (and embarrassing) ways, but before Bibot has a chance at a more lucrative second dream, his abused puppy gobbles up the remaining fruit. Marcel's dream is appropriately vengeful and ironic. This is a terrific read-aloud and the exuberantly detailed illustrations will keep readers enthralled.

C.P.S.

Instead of presenting kings and queens, magicians, or a family of dragons, Sylvia Waugh has created a family of rag dolls that come to life! They are a quaint little family who reside in England. They could be anyone's next door neighbors until a closer look is taken. Even though these characters are stitched, and one is even blue, they become lifelike and good friends before the series is over. Waugh has created a real treasure of a family for her readers.

Waugh, Sylvia
Mennyms in the Wilderness

Greenwillow Books. 1995.   ISBN: 0-688-13820-9. 254 p.

At first glance, the Mennyms seem to be an ordinary family, with parents, grandparents, children, and even a nanny. A closer look, though, reveals that the Mennyms are actually a family of life-size rag dolls! They live in London and pass their days acting human, hoping that no one will ever discover their secret. Will the Mennyms be found out when the city comes to build a highway through their neighborhood, and the Mennyms have to move? Middle readers will delight in this endearing addition to the tales of sometimes quirky life in the Mennym household.

Series/Sequels: *The Mennyms; Mennyms Alone; Mennyms in the Wilderness; Mennyms Under Siege; Mennyms Alive*

B.D.V.

Waugh, Sylvia
Mennyms Under Siege

Greenwillow. 1996.   ISBN: 0688143725. 219 p.

Pilbeam, the teen in the Mennym family, is bored and decides to go to town and attend the theater. A seemingly innocent act, though, does not go unnoticed by the townspeople. Now the Mennyms must band together to keep the neighbors at bay. There is some sadness in the Mennyms plight this time, but middle readers and already committed fans will be touched by this heartwarming tale, and ready to read more about the Mennyms.

Series/Sequels: *The Mennyms; Mennyms Alone; Mennyms in the Wilderness; Mennyms Under Siege; Mennyms Alive*

B.D.V.

Waugh, Sylvia
Mennyms Alive

Greenwillow. 1997.   ISBN: 0688152015. 224 p.

When the Mennym family is taken by the woman who owns the antique shop, they have a new home in an upstairs room of her store. The Mennyms, though, are still not safe, nor are they free until they can move to a new place. There, the Destiny of the Mennyms will be known and forever guaranteed. Middle readers will be touched and satisfied with Waugh's fitting conclusion for this likeable family.

Series/Sequels: *The Mennyms; Mennyms Alone; Mennyms in the Wilderness; Mennyms Under Siege; Mennyms Alive*

B.D.V.

J ane Yolen has written both beautiful new fairy tales and classic retellings of the older fairy tales. Here she has given her readers a trilogy that may appear small in size, but will speak volumes about the early years of Merlin, an area that hasn't yet received much attention in this legend.

Yolen, Jane
Passager: The Young Merlin Trilogy

Harcourt Brace. 1996.   ISBN: 0-15-200391-6. 76 p.

It has been a year since the eight-year-old boy was abandoned in the woods of medieval England. He has felt terror and hunger as he learned to fend for himself, becoming like one of the wild animals in the woods. One day, he sees a fascinating man with an independent, intelligent bird. When he follows them, the boy is captured by the falconer, who tames the boy and reteaches him the things he has lost. One night, in a dramatic incident, the falconer learns the boy's true name: Merlin. Yolen captures the magic of the fifteen-century-old Merlin story in *Passager*, the first in this lively trilogy.

Series/Sequels: The Young Merlin Trilogy: *Passager; Hobby; Merlin*

L.W.

Yolen, Jane
Hobby: The Young Merlin Trilogy, Book 2

Harcourt Brace. 1996.   ISBN: 0152008152. 90 p.

Young Merlin is twelve when the second book in the trilogy opens. The first scene describes how Merlin's adoptive family dies in a fire. Merlin, who now calls himself Hawk, is left with nothing and must set out on his own. First, he is taken prisoner by a frightful character named Fowler. When he escapes, he joins a crew from a traveling magic show. This dubious band of players doesn't treat Hawk as an equal, and instead uses his power to see into the future. Even though this book is slim in appearance, middle and older readers are definitely the intended audience for this sophisticated, yet engrossing story about the Arthurian legend. Don't miss the second book in this powerful trilogy.

Series Sequels: The Young Merlin Trilogy: *Passager; Hobby; Merlin*

B.D.V.

Yolen, Jane
Merlin: The Young Merlin Trilogy, Book 3

Harcourt Brace. 1997.   ISBN: 0152008144. 112 p.

In this final chapter to Yolen's captivating trilogy, young Merlin, now known as Hawk-Hobby, has returned to the forest to hide. There, he sets up camp with the wode-house, or wild folk, who live with the wolves. Hawk-Hobby escapes from these creatures with the help of a little boy named Cub, and they become friends and companions. By the end of the story, the readers know that Cub is the famed King Arthur in this beautiful story about the beginnings of the Arthurian legend. For the older readers who find this enchanting story, they will be richly rewarded.

Series/Sequels: The Young Merlin Trilogy: *Passager*; *Hobby*; *Merlin*

B.D.V.

Fairy Tales

Levine, Gail Carson
Ella Enchanted

HarperCollins. 1997.   ISBN: 0-06-027510-3. 232 p.

When Ella of Frell was born, the fairy Lucinda bestowed upon her the gift of obedience. The gift becomes a curse because she can never be herself, and there are those who would command her to do things that go against her sense of right. In a world inhabited by princes, ogres, giants, wicked stepsisters, and fairy godmothers, Ella struggles to break Lucinda's spell. Readers will relish this fantasy, which retells the Cinderella story in new and delightful ways.

Awards: Newbery Medal Honor Book, 1998; ALA Notable Books for Children, 1998; ALA Best Books for Young Adults, 1998

L.W.

McKinley, Robin
Rose Daughter

Greenwillow Books. 1997.   ISBN: 0-688-15439-5. 306 p.

Twenty years ago, readers were drawn to *Beauty*, Robin McKinley's exquisite retelling of her favorite fairy tale of "Beauty and the Beast." Now a new generation will experience the same wonder in her completely different version of the tale. Beauty and her two memorable sisters, Jeweltongue and Lionheart, move from the city to Rose Cottage after their mother dies and their father loses his wealth and position. From this setting, the tale unfolds. The beauty and intricacy of the language and the story will enchant the special reader.

Awards: ALA Best Books for Young Adults, 1998

Series/Sequels: *Beauty*; *Rose Daughter*

L.W.

Napoli, Donna Jo
Zel

Dutton Children's Books. 1996.   ISBN: 0-525-45612-0. 227 p.

This novel-length retelling of the Rapunzel story centers not only on the young girl trapped in her tower, but also on the prince who loves her and the mother who put her there. Part fairy tale and part psychological drama, it is a sobering, often dark, exploration of how despair and unfulfilled desire corrupt. Sure to be compared to Robin McKinley's *Beauty* and Gail Carson Levine's *Ella Enchanted*, though this is perhaps a less romantic and less accessible work. Nevertheless, young women enraptured by fairy tales will be sad when this book ends.

C.P.S.

Pyle, Howard; Trina Schart Hyman, illus.
PB Bearskin

Morrow Junior Books. 1997.   ISBN: 0-688-09837-1. Unpaged.

Hyman has illustrated this delightful fairy tale by Howard Pyle so that it can be shared with several age levels. On one level, this is simply the story about the miller's son who slays the dragon to marry the king's daughter. Hyman's illustrations have expanded the audience for this story, though, by showing a land where people of all different races live together in peace. Hyman's illustrations are not only beautiful to see, but also thought-provoking in their presentation of the possibilities of all races living and working together. The story and pictures provide a lively read-aloud for an older group.

B.D.V.

Short Stories

Ellis, Sarah
Back of Beyond: Stories of the Supernatural

Margaret K. McElderry. 1996.   ISBN: 0-689-81484-4. 136 p.

A collection of twelve short stories that explore supernatural occurrences in an otherwise natural world. The stories include a visit to a mansion later found not to have been built yet, an attack in a deserted parking lot thwarted by a mysterious apparition, and the inexplicable return of a knife lost at sea years before. Dramatic tension and fine writing distinguish these stories, which will be enjoyed by readers seeking something strange. Reluctant short-story readers should give these a try.

C.P.S.

The following book is a very special collection of fairy tales written by the old master, Carl Sandburg, that had not been available to the public until this book was published.

Sandburg, Carl; Paul Zelinsky, illus.
More Rootabagas

Alfred A. Knopf. 1993.   ISBN: 0-679-800700-0. 94 p.

This is a collection of ten never-before-published short stories for children, written in the 1920s. Sandburg bemoaned the lack of original American fairy tales and set about writing his own. They were ostensibly written for his own daughters, but any children used to old-fashioned stories and who delight in word play, nonsensical plots, and the sounds of words might enjoy this collection. Superbly illustrated by Caldecott medallist Zelinsky in colored pencil, these stories might be most successful when read aloud.

C.P.S.

Turner, Megan Whalen
Instead of Three Wishes

Greenwillow Books. 1995.   ISBN: 0-688-13922-1. 132 p.

A collection of seven glorious stories dealing with the supernatural and the fantastical. Whether the story is about time travel back to prehistoric Sweden, where the inhabitants of a small village are being driven mad by roaches; or an elf prince's futile attempts to pay back a debt, the author never fails to offer suspenseful, witty, and often provocative tales. A thoroughly enjoyable collection that should convince even the most skeptical reader that short stories can be great entertainment.

C.P.S.

Wyeth, Sharon Dennis; Curtis E. James, illus.
Vampire Bugs: Stories Conjured from the Past

Delacorte Press. 1995.   ISBN: 0-385-32082-5. 76 p.

There are six original, spooky tales, inspired by African American history and folklore, in this collection that focuses on the supernatural and the unexplainable. Whether describing the origins of fireflies or the capturing of hags in bottles held securely with nine-needle corks, the author succeeds in creating dark, chilling tales. Though this book may not be as accessible as some other, wildly popular short story collections, sophisticated readers will enjoy reading these tales on dark, stormy nights.

C.P.S.

Science Fiction

Bechard, Margaret
Star Hatchling

Viking. 1995.   ISBN: 0-670-861 49-9. 152 p.

Sem and Cheko, two ordinary(?!), claw-snapping, tongue-flicking young creatures who live on another planet, see a star falling from the sky and crashing into a clearing. They witness a different sort of creature emerge from the star, a creature that looks nothing like anything that lives on their planet! This is science fiction at its cleverest, as the young human is actually the alien who lands on a planet much different from Earth. The characters in each chapter alternate between the other-world creatures and the alien human, in a catchy, creative tale that just might happen in the future. It makes a side-splitting read for younger science fiction fans.

B.D.V.

Brennan, Herbie
The Mystery Machine

Margaret K. McElderry. 1995.   ISBN: 0-689-50615-5. 91 p.

Hubert is playing with his soccer ball when he accidentally kicks it into Mrs. Pomfrey-Parkinson's yard. She is the mean old woman who has moved in next door, and she yells at anyone who gets in her yard. This neighbor, though, seems to be more than just ornery. Her eyes begin flashing red when she is angry, and she appears to be hiding a strange, throbbing machine in her garden shed. Through an amazing set of circumstances, Hubert gets inside the garden shed, where he sees a glowing machine that is almost alive. Middle readers will delight in this clever story about extraterrestrials, as they find that getting to the alien is half the fun.

B.D.V.

Dexter, Catherine
Alien Game

Morrow Junior Books. 1995.   ISBN: 0-688-11332-X. 208 p.

On the eve of the annual school game, Elimination, played by tagging, or "killing" other students, mysterious Christina appears. She claims to have been a former student who moved away and has now returned, but Zoe has no recollection of her ever having lived in the area. Attempts to find old class pictures to support Christina's claim are thwarted when the photos literally go up in smoke. Zoe finally uncovers the truth—that Christina is an alien bent on transporting students back to her home—but no one will believe her. A creepy page-turner.

C.P.S.

Haddix, Margaret Peterson
Running Out of Time

Simon & Schuster Books for Young Readers. 1995.   ISBN: 0-689-80084. 185 p.

When her nineteenth-century town is devastated by an incurable illness, Jessie is stunned to learn from her mother that she is actually living in 1996. Her community, which was founded as an historic, and later scientific, experiment, has now become a virtual prison under constant surveillance by armed guards. It is up to Jessie, armed with an old pair of her mother's jeans and sketchy information about how to navigate in the industrialized world, to escape and find medical help. This is an exciting blend of fantasy and historical fiction that will keep children engaged.

C.P.S.

Howarth, Lesley
Weather Eye

Candlewick Press. 1995.   ISBN: 0-7636-0243-4 (pbk). 224 p.

The year is 1999, and in London, thirteen-year-old Telly is alarmed by the drastic weather changes that are occurring throughout the world. After Telly recovers from a severe concussion that seems to have heightened her senses, she realizes that she must act quickly and warn others of the impending danger to the planet. Using her computer, she alerts weather watchers in her school and around the world to the severity of the problem, and creates feelings of awareness and sensitivity toward the care of the planet. This is good science fiction with a message for older readers.

B.D.V.

Jennings, Patrick
Faith and the Electric Dogs

Scholastic. 1996.   ISBN: 0-590-69768-4. 146 p.

Faith is supremely unhappy at her California mama's decision to pull up stakes and settle in Chiapas, Mexico. Not only does everything seem different, but she's also having the devil of a time learning the lingo. Luckily, Edison, a street-wise, hip-hop, multilingual *perro caliente* enters her life by saving her from the school bully. Together they ride off in a homemade rocket, hoping to find nirvana, or at least California. Everything in this breezy novel is slightly off-kilter, but readers willing to suspend a lot of disbelief will find it fun. Spanish (and some canine) can be learned by reading the wacky margins.

C.P.S.

Klause, Annette Curtis
Alien Secrets

Delacorte Press. 1993.   ISBN: 0-385-30928-7. 227 p.

Puck, a twelve-year-old who has been expelled from yet another boarding school, is on her way to Shoon where her parents are doing alien research. While on board the spaceship *Cat's Cradle*, she becomes involved in intergalactic espionage when she tries to help her friend Hush retrieve the artifact that signifies freedom to his alien race. If she fails, neither Puck nor Hush can return to Shoon with dignity. The story has enough heroes, villains, ghosts, action, and danger to keep eager readers turning the pages as rapidly as possible.

L.W.

Lowry, Lois
The Giver

Bantam Doubleday Dell. 1994.   ISBN: 0-440-40087-2. 180 p.

Jonas's life had been perfect for the first eleven years. There were no wars, no violence, and no fear of pain. All decisions in his life, and in his country, had already been made. When Jonas turned twelve, though, he, like all children, was assigned the job that he would perform for the rest of his life. Jonas was to study with the Giver, the one person responsible for keeping all the memories of life. Jonas would learn about the happiness of life, but he would also experience heartache, misery, devastation, and finally loneliness. Would this knowledge change Jonas's life forever? Lowry's remarkable book about freedom in another world is a powerful read that will be cherished forever by middle and adult readers alike.

> **Awards:** Newbery Medal Book, 1994; ALA Best Books for Young Adults,1994; ALA Notable Books for Children, 1994

B.D.V.

Time Travel

Banks, Lynne Reid, James Watling, illus.
The Key to the Indian

Avon Books. 1998   ISBN: 0-380-97717-6. 228 p.

Now that Omri's father knows about the plastic figures who come to life in Omri's secret cupboard, they must both work together to get back to the 1800s. The fate of Little Bear and the other Iroquois Indians rests in their hands, if only they can figure out a way to transport themselves back to Little Bear and his time. Their best laid plans go terribly awry, though, when magic is added to their car key. Omri and his brother Gillon mistakenly travel to India where Omri's great-grandfather resides, while Omri's father sets off on a separate adventure all his own!

Banks takes both old and new readers of The Indian in the Cupboard series on a ride of their lives as they stumble into different times and places from the past. The fifth book in this series is filled with just as much humor, intrigue and adventure as her last novels, while the story itself takes some new and unexpected turns into the past. Another lively story for middle grade readers from Lynne Reid Banks.

> **Series/Sequels:** *The Indian in the Cupboard*; *The Return of the Indian*; *The Secret of the Indian*; *The Mystery of the Cupboard*; *The Key to the Indian*

B.D.V.

Conrad, Pam
Zoe Rising

HarperCollins. 1996.   ISBN: 0-06-027217-1. 131 p.

Zoe is spending the summer at camp when she begins to experience troubling out-of-body episodes, much as she did years before. Zoe realizes that she's entering the childhood of her emotionally disturbed mother, and that she alone can alter the past to allow her mother to escape the physical abuse suffered at the hands of an evil man. This is a well-written sequel to *Stonewords* and should engage younger readers who aren't yet sophisticated enough to tackle more demanding time-travel fantasy.

> **Series/Sequels:** *Stonewords*; *Zoe Rising*

C.P.S.

Farmer, Nancy
The Ear, the Eye, and the Arm

Puffin Books. 1994.   ISBN: 0-14-037641-0. 311 p.

In 2194,Tendai, Rita, and Kuda escape from their high-security, luxurious home in Zimbabwe to see the real world. Their parents quickly hire the Ear, the Eye, and the Arm, detectives with paranormal abilities, to track down the missing children. The detectives' mission takes them to Cow's Guts, the city's seamiest area, where the children have been captured by the fearsome She Elephant and made into slaves mining toxic waste to find rare plastics. The children stay just out of reach of the detectives until the story's climax on top of the Mile High MacIlwaine Hotel. The history of Zimbabwe is skillfully interwoven in this tale of a futuristic world of fantasy and adventure.

L.W.

Fleischman, Sid; Peter Sis, illus.
The 13th Floor: A Ghost Story

Greenwillow Books. 1995.   ISBN: 0-688-14216-8. 134 p.

Twelve-year-old Buddy finds an old ship's trumpet that belonged to a relative of his from the seventeenth century. For fun, Buddy calls to this departed relative, who was known to be the captain of a pirate ship. Later that day, Buddy receives a strange message on the family's answering machine and realizes that his sister, Liz, has disappeared. When Buddy goes to look for her in an old building, he stops the elevator on the thirteenth floor and steps onto a pirate ship that existed 300 years ago! Young and middle readers will delight in accompanying Buddy on this zany story of time travel, comedy, and adventure.

B.D.V.

Peck, Richard
Lost in Cyberspace

Dial Books for Young Readers. 1995.   ISBN: 1-8037-1931-0. 151 p.

Josh Lewis and his best friend, Aaron Zimmer, are sixth-graders at Huckley School for Boys in New York City. Aaron is a computer whiz and uses the school media center's computers as a time machine. Suddenly he and Josh find themselves in the library of a house in 1923, and some of the people living in that house find themselves propelled into the future. This fast-paced story, filled with cyber lingo, will satisfy die-hard fans of time travel while also appealing to others as a good read.

L.W.

Paperback Science Fiction Series

Series: Animorphs

Author: Applegate, K. A.

Publisher: Scholastic

Jake, Marco, Tobias, Rachel, and Cassie were taking a shortcut home when they saw it: a bright light in the sky that was coming straight toward them. That was the night their lives changed forever. Now they can "morph" into any animal shape, so that they can defend the world against interplanetary takeover. This popular series details their struggle.

Titles:
1. *The Invasion*
2. *The Visitor*
3. *The Encounter*
4. *The Message*
5. *The Predator*
6. *The Capture*
7. *The Stranger*
8. *The Alien*
9. *The Secret*
10. *The Android*
11. *The Forgotten*
12. *The Reaction*
13. *The Change*
14. *The Unknown*
15. *The Escape*
16. *The Warning*
17. *The Underground*
18. *The Decision*
19. *The Departure*
20. *The Discovery*
21. *The Threat*
22. *The Solution*
23. *The Pretender*
24. *The Suspicion*
25. *The Extreme*
26. *The Attack*
27. *The Exposed*
28. *The Experiment*
29. *The Sickness*
30. *The Reunion*
31. *The Conspiracy*
32. *The Separation*
33. *The Illusion*
34. *The Prophecy*
35. *The Prophecy*
36. *The Mutation*
37. *The Weakness*
38. *Andalite Chronicles*
39. *Visser*

40. *Hork-Bajir Chronicles*
41. *Megamorphs #1: The Andalite's Gift*
42. *Megamorphs #2*
43. *Megamorphs #3*
44. *Meet the Stars of Animorphs*
45. *Alternamorphs*

The Authors' All-Time Favorite Fantasy and Science Fiction Stories

Babbitt, Natalie—**Tuck Everlasting**

Cooper, Susan—**The Dark Is Rising**

Lewis, C.S.—**The Chronicles of Narnia**

Lowry, Lois—**The Giver**

McKinley, Robin—**Beauty: A Retelling of the Story of Beauty and the Beast**

McKinley, Robin—**The Blue Sword**

Morpurgo, Michael—**King of the Cloud Forests**

Price, Susan—**The Ghost Drum: A Cat's Tale**

Pullman, Philip—**The Golden Compass**

Chapter 6

Historical Fiction

Good historical fiction for young people can be a real gold mine for readers in search of a fulfilling genre, if the excellent choices that are available are well presented. Sometimes high-quality historical fiction is passed over because young people don't realize that these spirited accounts exist. The stories are packed with action, suspense, mystery, and even humor; they'll get readers motivated and keep them involved. While being captivated by a thrilling plot line, the readers are also learning about a specific event or period in history.

Historical fiction isn't merely a recounting of history, though. It is a presentation of an event from the past from an entirely new perspective. The author, who is living today, brings new information to the topic because of the passage of time, thus giving new insight and an entirely different interpretation to the event. The story, or plot line, is already well defined because an actual time and setting form the basis of the story. The focus is on characters from the period, or on the period itself, and the fictionalized part of the story develops from these already well-defined facts. The tale is usually presented through the eyes of a young person who is living through and experiencing the events of the time, but the actual story is shaped by the author, who has researched the material and gives an accurate account of the incident, though from a different viewpoint. Ultimately, both authors and readers are rewarded by gaining this new perspective on history. The stories listed here are filled with so much drama and excitement that readers will forget that they are also a lesson in history.

Anglo-Saxon Period

Sutcliff, Rosemary
The Shining Company
Farrar, Straus & Giroux. 1990.   ISBN: 0-374358074. 296 p.

King Mynyddog is assembling 300 men to fight the invading Saxons in A.D. 600 Young Prosper becomes shieldbearer to Prince Gorth as the 300 train for a year before going to war. This story of adventure and heroism is based on *The Gododdin*, the earliest surviving North British poem, which celebrates the death of a band of British warriors. Fans of Arthurian legend and diehard historical fiction buffs will, no doubt, be enthralled by this tale of another time.

L.W.

Middle Ages

Blackwood, Gary
The Shakespeare Stealer
Dutton Children's Books. 1998.   ISBN: 0-525-45863-8. 216 p.

The year was 1587, and few people could read, let alone take shorthand. Surprisingly, the twelve-year-old orphan named Widge could do both. When Simon Bass, a shady character in the theater world, realized the money to be made from Widge's talents, he quickly purchased the orphan for his personal gain. He planned to have Widge transcribe a popular play while it was being presented, so that Bass could sell it illegally to other performing troupes. Widge, though, liked the theater troupe and didn't want to rob his newfound friends. Here is an exciting swashbuckler filled with twists, turns, and surprises that will leave middle-grade readers, especially boys, guessing to the very end.

B.D.V.

Karen Cushman is a masterful storyteller and a popular, prize-winning author. The female characters in her next two books are everything young people want to see: strong, intelligent, forward-thinking, with just the right amount of humor. Cushman's books are enjoyed by everyone, but girls especially love to read about these clever young girls who were centuries ahead of their time.

Cushman, Karen
Catherine, Called Birdy
Clarion Books. 1994.   ISBN: 0-395-68186-3. 160 p.

Thirteen-year-old Catherine, who is known as Birdy, must keep a journal. Her brother has instructed her to do this in the hopes of making her less childish. Birdy will do this only if the task takes the place of spinning. She hates to waste her time learning the humdrum duties of a lady; feisty Birdy, with a mind of her own, would rather be a painter, a juggler, a peddler, or anything but a lady whose only fate is to be forced into the bonds of marriage. Cushman's story of Birdy, presented as a diary, brings this time in history to life. Birdy's descriptions of her days over a year's time are filled with priceless bits of humor, insight, and charm. All readers will delight as Birdy figures out how to make the best of her situation.

Awards: ALA Notable Books for Children, 1995

B.D.V.

Cushman, Karen
The Midwife's Apprentice

Clarion Books. 1995.   ISBN: 0395-69229-6. 122 p.

A scrawny young girl, no more than twelve or thirteen years old, was found in the barn sleeping in a heap of dung for warmth. Jane, the town midwife, keeps the child, to get as much work from her as she can, but the girl realizes that she has finally found a place to live. It wasn't to be an easy life: Jane called the girl Beetle and treated her poorly, but Beetle began to learn the life of a midwife's apprentice, and her skills and self-confidence grew enough for her to reward herself with the name of Alyce. Cushman's award-winning novel paints a rowdy, colorful picture of life in the Middle Ages. The feisty and intelligent character of Alyce will have middle- and upper-grade readers cheering on every page.

Awards: Newbery Medal Honor Book, 1996; ALA Notable Books for Children, 1996; ALA Best Books for Young Adults, 1996

B.D.V.

Haugaard, Erik Christian
The Revenge of the Forty-seven Samurai

Houghton Mifflin. 1995.   ISBN: 0-395-70809-5. 226 p.

In the time when the Shogun ruled Japan, and the samurai warriors were the most respected members of society, Jiro was a lowly servant to one of the brave samurai. He is just a young boy, but he is chosen as his master's spy during an elaborate plan to avenge the unjust death of Lord Asano. Jiro calls himself a "fly on the wall" as he learns when to talk and when to listen, in this intricate but exciting adventure novel set in feudal Japan. Readers will be caught up in Jiro's world and his questions about the society in which he lives.

Awards: ALA Notable Books for Children, 1996

L.W.

Here are two books by Frances Temple, both set in the thirteenth century but each worlds apart from the other. Both stories are about the upcoming weddings of the characters, but there the similarities end. Temple describes life in Arabia at that time, filled with sheiks, battling tribes, and the magic of the desert. Temple then moves to England and sends the betrothed on a quest to Spain. Whether fast-paced with page-turning adventures, or a monumental trek across countries where many characters appear to spin their tales, these books give older readers a real taste for life at that time.

Temple, Frances
6-8 The Beduin's Gazelle

Orchard. 1996.　　　　　　　　　　　　　　　　　　ISBN: 0-531-09519-3. 150 p.

The year is 1302, or 680 according to the Muslim calendar. The young and beautiful Halima is falling asleep, dreaming about her upcoming marriage to Atiyah. Suddenly she is awakened by Atiyah, who tells her that he must run away or be captured by a warring tribe that is coming to do battle. This is the beginning of Halima's and Atiyah's story of separation. One character is lost in the desert, while the other is sent to study in the city, and both are faced with the evil threats of Sheikh Raisulu. This is both a gripping tale of the characters' adventures and a well-researched, informative look at the world of Islam in the thirteenth century. It makes rich reading for older readers.

B.D.V.

Temple, Frances
6-8 The Ramsay Scallop

Orchard. 1994.　　　　　　　　　　　　　　　　　　ISBN: 0-531-08686-0. 310 p.

Elenor is a mere fourteen years old and she is already sad about life. She is to be married to Lord Thomas, who has been away battling in the Crusades—and what Elenor remembers of Thomas, she doesn't like. Elenor is afraid to be married, and Thomas is exhausted from the Crusades, and neither wants the next part of their lives to begin. Their priest, Father Gregory, sees the problem and sends the two on a pilgrimage to Spain. After their long travels, meetings, stories, and songs from a whole cast of characters, the two form a strong bond and look forward to their lives together. This story is slow going, but well worth the effort for older readers looking for an enchanting story of romance and intrigue.

Awards: ALA Best Books for Young Adults, 1995.

B.D.V.

The Renaissance

The Renaissance was truly the time in history when modern science, as we know it, appeared. It also marked the time when artistic and intellectual activity took on a physical role in this new, developing society.

Llorente, Pilar Molina. Translated from the Spanish by Juan Ramon Alonso
The Apprentice

Farrar, Straus & Giroux. 1993.　　　　　　　　　　　ISBN: 0-374-303894. 101 p.

Thirteen-year-old Arduino, the youngest son in a family of tailors in Renaissance Florence, longs to break with tradition and become a painter. His father arranges to have him apprenticed to Cosimodi Forli, an elderly artist with a horrible secret. Upon discovering a prisoner in the maestro's attic, Arduino's drive to become an artist collides with his desire to do right. His subsequent struggle toward an eventual happy ending forms the heart of this intriguing historical novel.

C.P.S.

Sixteenth Century and the Colonial Period

Dorris, Michael
Sees Behind Trees

Hyperion Books for Children. 1996.   ISBN: 0-7868-0224-3. 104 p

No matter how hard he tries, Walnut cannot shoot his arrows to meet the mark. He sees only blurred images, whereas the other boys can see things clearly. Walnut learns that he has special gifts when he uses other senses: smell, hearing, and touch. When it is time for the boys of the village to pass the test to become a man, Walnut "sees" in his own way and earns the name Sees Behind Trees. This lyrical, wise, and funny story, set in sixteenth-century America, shows how one boy turns a challenge into a special gift.

L.W.

Graham, Harriet
A Boy and His Bear

Margaret K. McElderry. 1996.   ISBN: 0-689-80943-3. 196 p.

After the death of his father, Dickon is forced to become a tanner's apprentice in Elizabethan London. There he sees a bear cub, separated from its mother and transported to the city to be used in bearbaiting, a cruel and popular sport of the time. Given the task of caring for the cub, because of the unusual attachment the two have formed, Dickon is determined to save the animal from certain death. Children will enjoy the sweet relationship between the boy and the beast, and be intrigued by life in this fascinating time. Give this one to readers who profess dislike for historical fiction.

C.P.S.

Seventeenth Century

6

Fleischman, Paul
Saturnalia

Harper & Row. 1990.   ISBN: 0-06-021912-2. 113 p.

The year is 1681 in Boston, six years after the Narraganset Indian tribe is almost totally destroyed in an ambush. Fourteen-year-old William is one of the few tribesmen to be taken prisoner, and is sent to live among the townspeople to learn a trade. He lives with the goodhearted Currie family and becomes a printer, but he never forgets his tribe and continues to search for his lost brother. When Saturnalia arrives, the topsy-turvy holiday when people can trade places with their opposites for a night, William comes upon two members from his tribe who are hiding in his village. Now William, and Fleischman's older readers looking for an involving tale, must choose the lifestyle William can pursue.

B.D.V.

Eighteenth Century

Krensky, Stephen; Madeline Sorel, illus.
The Printer's Apprentice

Delacorte Press. 1995.   ISBN: 0-385-32095-7. 103 p.

Gus Croft is ten years old and is fortunate to be an apprentice to the famous printer, William Bradford, in New York in 1734. Although Bradford supports the governor, Peter Zenger, a fellow printer, doesn't share those opinions, and makes no secret of it in his newspaper, *The New York Weekly Journal*. Zenger is put in jail for printing scandalous opinions about His Majesty's governor. Gus begins to question whether it is fair for people with different ideas to be put in prison. This novel is a lively mix of history and fiction for younger readers.

L.W.

Unfortunately, slavery had already been well established all over the world long before the eighteenth century. Here are two examples of how ingrained it was, from two different continents.

Rinaldi, Ann
Wolf by the Ears

Scholastic. 1991.   ISBN: 0-590-04341-3. 272 p.

Harriet Hemings, the illegitimate daughter of Thomas Jefferson, narrates this compelling account of what life was like living at Monticello in two worlds. On the one hand, Harriet was treated as a member of the upper class: tutored in math and literature and taught domestic arts. On the other hand, she was expected to work as a slave and to address her father as "Master." When a chance to leave presents itself, with the assurances of freedom but at the cost of passing for white, Harriet is torn between love and loyalty to her heritage and the desire to live without constraints. A fascinating, albeit fictionalized, examination of an important time in American history and a woman's struggle to stay true to herself.

C.P.S.

Shaik, Fatima
Melitte

Dial Books for Young Readers. 1997.   ISBN: 0-8037-2106-4. 147 p.

Melitte doesn't know her mother or father. She only knows the French couple who have held her prisoner on their farm in Louisiana for as long as she can remember. When the couple has a baby, though, and Melitte is given the job of supervision, she learns what love for another person is all about. Melitte raises Marie and teaches her the truth about slavery. When Melitte is thirteen and the two girls are to be separated, they must decide if it is better to have a true friend or to own property through slavery. This story describes the crimes of slavery that were occurring in the United States by the mid-1700s. It is an informative and realistic look at history, for older readers looking for facts on slavery.

B.D.V.

Yolen, Jane; David Shannon, illus.
The Ballad of the Pirate Queens

Harcourt Brace. 1995.   ISBN: 0-15-200710-5. Unpaged.

Anne Bonney and Mary Reade were the most famous female pirates who sailed the seas in the 1700s. This ballad recounts the legend of these women, who bravely fought the men from the battleship *Albion*. They were the only crew members on deck guarding the pirate ship *Vanity* when it was overtaken by the *Albion*; the rest of the crew was drinking and carousing below deck and never heard the women's cries for help. David Shannon's illustrations bring this story to life, while Yolen's closing notes leave readers wondering what really happened. Strong female characters make this a lively read-aloud picture book for older readers.

Awards: ALA Notable Books for Children, 1996

B.D.V.

Nineteenth Century and Frontier Life

Anderson, Margaret J.; Marie Le Glatin Keis, illus.
Children of Summer: Henri Fabre's Insects

Farrar, Straus & Giroux. 1997.   ISBN: 0-374-31243-5. 100 p.

This is a fictionalized biography of nineteenth-century French entomologist Henri Fabre, whose fieldwork rarely strayed beyond his own backyard, and whose assistants were frequently his own children. This book might have worked better as a straight biography; it lacks some of the elements of good fiction writing, such as character development and a sustained plot. Nonetheless, those lucky children who read it will be rewarded by fascinating descriptions of various insects and the methodology used by this brilliant and very patient scientist.

C.P.S.

Anderson, Rachel
Black Water

Henry Holt. 1995.   ISBN: 0-8050-3847-7. 168 p.

Albert, a boy who lives with his mother in nineteenth-century England, experiences lapses of memory. When he was younger, Albert's mother told him that these were times when he would slip into "pretty dreams." Now that Albert is growing into adolescence, though, these missing periods get longer, more violent, and frightening for Albert and everyone around him. Over time, Albert comes to realize that he has epilepsy, an uncontrollable illness at that time. Anderson tells a difficult, yet thought-provoking and ultimately rewarding, story about learning to live and prosper in society against apparently insurmountable odds.

B.D.V.

Armstrong, Jennifer; Emily Martindale, illus.
Black-Eyed Susan

Crown. 1995. ISBN: 0-517-70107-3. 120 p.

The time is the latter half of the nineteenth century, and ten-year-old Susie and her parents have moved to the prairies of South Dakota. Susie and her father think the wide open spaces are just fine for them, but Susie's mother finds the landscape and everything else just too big, too wide, and too overwhelming. As Susie's mother becomes more depressed, it appears that the family will have to return to Ohio, where life was easier. Luckily, a family of homesteaders passes through and changes the look of prairie life. Armstrong's presentation is reminiscent of *Sarah, Plain and Tall*, and is perfect for younger readers.

B.D.V.

Auch, Mary Jane
Journey to Nowhere

Henry Holt. 1997. ISBN: 0-8050-4922-3. 202 p.

It is 1815, and eleven-year-old Remembrance—Mem for short—is leaving her home in Connecticut to move with her family to New York. They sell all their belongings, except for what will fit in a covered wagon, and begin their travels through the heavily wooded wilderness. The family must struggle with the hardships of nature and the loneliness of separation to reach the new land. The story shows how some settlers contended with bears, mountain lions, floods, and forests so thick the sunlight would disappear, rather than crossing the prairies to the West. It is high adventure, with a new slant on homesteading, for middle readers.

B.D.V.

Here is another book by Avi, this time a real page-turner in the historical fiction genre.

Avi
The Barn

Orchard. 1994. ISBN: 0-531-06861-7. 106 p.

When Ben is nine, he is sent away to school because he is very bright. One day, his teenage sister Nettie comes to take him back to the family farm in the Oregon Territory. His father has had a stroke, and Harrison, Nettie, and Ben must do the work. Ben gets the idea that if they can build a barn all by themselves, Father will recover. The children cut the trees, haul the logs, pile rocks for the foundation, and raise the walls and roof. Ben's dream cannot come true, but the barn becomes a gift to their dying father. Ben's narrative is poetic in this small, quiet book.

L.W.

Bunting, Eve; Ronald Himler, illus.
Train to Somewhere

Clarion Books. 1996. ISBN: 0-395-71325-0. 32 p.

It is the late 1800s, and Marianne joins thirteen other orphans on what is known as the Orphan Train, as they travel out West looking for families who will adopt them. This practice continued in the United States from the 1850s to the late 1920s, to alleviate the growing problem of homeless children in the East. This tale, though in picture-book format, is for older readers, and describes a heartwrenching solution to the orphan problem. The text is short, but the story and pictures are filled with emotions, as the homeless children find a resolution of sorts on the Orphan Train.

Awards: ALA Notable Books for Children, 1997

B.D.V.

Cushman, Karen
The Ballad of Lucy Whipple

Clarion Books. 1996.   ISBN: 0-395-72806-1. 197 p.

When her indomitable family heads out West, away from all of the comforts and refinements of life in Massachusetts, California Morning Whipple is not amused. In a series of whiny letters to her grandparents, begging them to save her from the indignities of frontier life, she describes her increasingly primitive (and exciting) life in the gold-mining town where her mother has set up shop. In a book filled with colorful characters and hijinks, the reader is swept along by good writing and admiration for this resourceful young woman, as she becomes increasingly aware that her new home is just the place for her.

C.P.S.

DeFelice, Cynthia
The Apprenticeship of Lucas Whitaker

Farrar, Straus & Giroux. 1996.   ISBN: 0-374-34669-0. 152 p.

In the nineteenth century, consumption was an almost certain death sentence, and Lucas watches helplessly as his entire family succumbs to the disease. He is taken in by Dr. Uriah Beecher and becomes the apprentice to this thoughtful and honorable man. When a controversial "cure" is found, which involves exhuming the consumption victim's body, burning the heart, and inhaling the smoke, Lucas feels that he won't be at peace until he discovers if this practice offers an end to so much suffering. This moving, engrossing novel was deservedly on several "best of the year" lists.

Awards: ALA Notable Books for Children, 1997

C.P.S.

DeFelice, Cynthia
Weasel

Avon. 1990.   ISBN: 0-380-71358-6. 119 p.

During the winter of 1839, eleven-year-old Nathan Fowler and his younger sister, Molly, learn that the legend of the monster Weasel is true. Although Weasel is not part man and part wild animal, as the story said, he is a bloodthirsty killer. Like his namesake, the weasel, he sleeps by day and hunts by night. Now he is stalking Nathan in the Ohio woods. History of the wilderness frontier and the removal of the Shawnee by the government are intertwined with a young boy's adventure in this accessible story for middle-grade readers.

L.W.

Dexter, Catherine
Safe Return

Candlewick Press. 1996.   ISBN: 0-7636-0005-9. 94 p.

This quiet, powerful story of love and family is based on a true story that occurred in 1824 on Gotland Island in the Baltic Sea. The story is told by Ursula, an orphan who lives with her Aunt Dana and Uncle Josef. The island is famous for its knitting, and every year women from the island sail to Stockholm to sell the hundreds of sweaters they have made. Ursula misses her aunt, and the worry grows with each day the ship is late returning home. On the day before Christmas, when everyone is convinced that the women will never return, the sails of the *Galatina* are seen coming into the harbor.

L.W.

Fleischman, Paul
The Borning Room

HarperCollins. 1991.   ISBN: 0-060-23762-7. 101 p.

Lying in the room where she was born in 1851, Georgina remembers her long life on the Ohio frontier. One room can tell the story of a family: a room where babies are born and the dying go to a better place. During this time, Ohio is divided between the abolitionists and the pro-slavery people. When young Georgina finds a terrified slave hiding in the cornfield, she knows that her family could be severely punished for hiding the runaway. She also knows that the work they are doing is very important. Babies continue to be born and loved ones to die in this slight book with great depth. Thoughtful readers will be touched by this quiet but powerful picture of life in another time.

L.W.

Hahn, Mary Downing
The Gentleman Outlaw and Me—Eli

Clarion Books. 1996.   ISBN: 0-395-73083-X. 212 p.

In 1887, Eliza Yates and her dog, Caesar, run away from cruel Aunt Mabel and Uncle Homer to look for Eliza's father in Tinville, Colorado. She becomes Elijah Bates and takes up with eighteen-year-old Calvin Thaddeus Featherbone, the Second, better known as the Gentleman Outlaw. His illegal schemes get them into numerous scrapes as they make their way to Colorado. Readers will root for spunky Eli during her adventures in the old West.

L.W.

Hall, Donald; Emily Arnold McCully, illus.
Old Home Day

Browndeer Press. 1996.   ISBN: 0-15-276896-3. 48 p.

Tens of thousands of years ago, the Ice Age formed what would eventually become Blackwater Pond. Around this body of water eventually sprang up a bustling village founded by Enoch Boswell. The author follows this New Hampshire town through cyclical changes of growth, decline, and eventual renewal over the course of 200 years, beginning in 1799. The watercolor illustrations by Caldecott Award-winner McCully are gorgeous. Upper elementary students will gain a better understanding of the interplay of humans and nature that has created the environment of the present.

C.P.S.

Holub, Josef
The Robber and Me

Henry Holt. 1997.   ISBN: 0-8050-5599-1. 213 p.

When the orphan boy, Boniface Schroll, is sent to live with his uncle, Emil Schroll, the trip alone should have told him that life would not be easy. He is left in the forest, where he becomes lost, terrified, and exhausted, until he is finally carried to his uncle's doorstep by a mysterious man in a black hat. Boniface learns that his uncle is cold and uncaring, and his schoolmaster turns out to be an equally wicked and cruel man. In fact, the only person with any good qualities is the man in the black hat, who is known throughout town as the robber. In an intricate, descriptive novel, skilled readers will admire a sad little boy who has the courage to speak up against overwhelming odds.

L.W.

Klass, Sheila Solomon
A Shooting Star: A Novel about Annie Oakley

Holiday House. 1996.   ISBN: 0-8234-1279-2. 173 p.

Phoebe Anne Moses, the girl who became Annie Oakley, didn't start out as a sharpshooter. Annie's father died when she was young, and out of desperation Annie's mother sent her to the country farm, the poorhouse for people who had no place else to go. After leaving there, Annie worked for an abusive family who beat her and kept her as a slave. When Annie finally escaped, she returned to her home to hunt and help feed her starving family. Never having taken to sewing, Annie found that sharpshooting was the life for her. This lively account will bring both laughter and tears to middle readers looking for an action-packed read.

B.D.V.

Myers, Anna
Graveyard Girl

Walker. 1995.   ISBN: 0-8027-8260-4. 125 p.

 6

When a yellow fever epidemic causes countless deaths in Memphis during 1878, Grace tolls the bell at the cemetery for each new dead soul. When ten-year-old Eli's mother and little sister die and his grieving father runs away, Eli vows to harden his heart against any further loss. Grace, the Graveyard Girl, and Addie, who is an orphan, begin to convince Eli that he might find happiness again. Finally the October frost ends the terrible epidemic and life begins to return to normal. Although the story is very sad, it captures the warmth and goodness of people during difficult times.

L.W.

Paterson, Katherine
Jip: His Story

Dutton Children's Books. 1996.   ISBN: 0-525-67543-4. 208 p.

As an infant, Jip is tossed from a rolling wagon and separated from his mother. His origins a mystery, he has spent his entire life working on a Vermont poor farm. When a new resident named Put arrives, caged like an animal because of periodic bouts of insanity, Jip cares for him and discovers that he has finally found a friend. A stranger's arrival in town, with dangerous information about Jip's family, forces him to realize that the only hope for safety lies in escape—yet how can he leave behind his new, helpless friend? This exquisitely written novel may encourage children to reflect on loyalty and honor.

> **Awards:** ALA Notable Books for Children, 1997; ALA Best Books for Young Adults, 1997

C.P.S.

Segal, Jerry; Dav Pilkey, illus.
The Place Where Nobody Stopped
Orchard. 1991.   ISBN: 0-531-05897-2. 154 p.

Once upon a time (1895) in Russia, there stood a town comprised of humble shacks so dilapidated and insignificant that people referred to it as " the place where nobody stopped." In this "non-town" lived a lonely, kindhearted baker named Yosip. Despite his many good deeds, he was always alone, until the glorious day when Mordecai Ben Yahbahbai and his family stopped to rest and stayed for the rest of their lives. This is a charming, humorous account of nine years in the lives of these characters. Despite numerous illustrations by the fantastically popular Pilkey, kids may have to be persuaded to give this old-fashioned, well-written folktale a try.

C.P.S.

Sis, Peter, au. and illus.
6-8 Small Tall Tale from the Far Far North
Alfred A. Knopf. 1993.   ISBN: 0-679-84345-0. Unpaged.

In an intriguing melding of text, maps, watercolors, and pen-and-ink drawings, we learn the story of Jan Welzl, a Czech folk hero. He left his hometown in the late 1800s and traveled to the frozen north, learning the ways of the Eskimos. When greedy Europeans invade the land seeking gold, Jan Welzl diverts them to a magnetic mountain so his friends can be protected. Because of the complexity of the text, this is a picture book for older readers. Its interesting prologue and epilogue tell more about the legend and the lifelong interest Peter Sis has had in the character of Jan Welzl.

L.W.

Valgardson, W. D.; Ian Wallace, illus.
Sarah and the People of Sand River
Groundwood Books. 1996.   ISBN: 0-88899-255-6. 44 p.

Sarah's best friends are Baldur the dog and Loki the raven. She and her father live in a little cabin on the shores of Lake Winnipeg in a place called New Iceland. When her father sends her far away to go to school, she is treated with great cruelty by the family who takes her in.. A mysterious raven and a native man and woman bring her magic gifts that help her to survive. Based on a true story of people from Iceland who settled among the Cree in Manitoba in the late 1800s, this beautiful story is much like a fairy tale. Rich text and lovely illustrations make history come alive.

L.W.

Weitzman, David, au. and illus.
Old Ironsides: Americans Build a Fighting Ship

Houghton Mifflin. 1997.   ISBN: 0-395-74678-7. 32 p.

The thirty-two-page picture-book format is quite deceiving in this story of the building of the *Constitution*, America's first fighting ship. From the initial drawings about the selection of wood, every step of how the ship was built is described and illustrated with detailed line drawings. The saga of the building of the ship is seen through the eyes of young John Aylwin. Except for this fictional character, this book could be considered nonfiction. It recounts a fascinating and little-known story from American history.

L.W.

Yep, Laurence
Dragon's Gate

HarperCollins. 1993.   ISBN: 0-060-22971-3. 273 p.

Otter wants to join his father and uncle and work in America, the Land of the Golden Mountain. His mother disagrees, though, until Otter must either flee his homeland of China, or stay and be wrongfully accused of murder. The year is 1867, and the Chinese are helping to build the first transcontinental railroad in the United States. Otter meets up with the other workers as they blast their way through the Sierra Nevada Mountains, and he quickly learns that survival will be his biggest challenge in this new country. Yep's award-winning novel shows how, against all odds, the Chinese labor force was crucial in building part of history. This survival tale is not to be missed by older readers looking for excitement.

Awards: Newbery Medal Honor Book, 1994; ALA Notable Books for Children, 1993

Series/Sequels: *Dragonwings*; *The Serpent's Children*; *Mountain Light*; *Dragon's Gate* (prequel)

B.D.V.

Slavery and the Civil War

Armstrong, Jennifer
Steal Away

Orchard. 1992.   ISBN: 0-531-0598-39. 207 p.

In 1855, the fates of two young girls, one white and one black, collide and change both lives forever. When Susannah is orphaned and has to go live with a remote uncle in Virginia, she is appalled to be given Bethlehem Reid, a young slave, as a gift. Although friendship is hard to build between the two, mutual need and misery compel them to form an alliance to escape to the North. Their harrowing tale is recounted forty-one years later, when Susannah visits a dying Beth and they both come to realize that the bond forged so many years before is unbreakable. A fine novel about slavery.

C.P.S.

The next story is not about slavery in the United States. Instead, it moves to Africa to show how the horrors of slavery began.

Berry, James
Ajeemah and His Son

HarperCollins. 1991.   ISBN: 0-0621043-5. 83 p.

The year is 1807, and the slave trade is reaching its peak. Slave traders are making a fortune selling Africans to willing buyers in Britain, the Caribbean, and the Americas. Ajeemah and his eighteen-year-old son, Atu, are innocently walking to the home of Sisi, Atu's bride-to-be, to leave the dowry with her father. Suddenly, Ajeemah and Atu are ambushed, captured, and sold to two different farms in Jamaica. Father and son spend the rest of their days separated from one another, unknowingly held prisoner a mere two miles apart. Berry has given his readers a telling look at the atrocity and inhumanity of slavery. It is a hard-hitting account that middle readers will not soon forget.

   Awards: Boston Globe-Horn Book Award, 1993

B.D.V.

Haas, Jessie
Westminster West

Greenwillow Books. 1997.   ISBN: 0-688-14883-2. 168 p.

After an illness leaves younger sister Clare prone to imagining herself delicate, Sue is resentful of the added chores that she must perform around the farm. Added to her problems is the tension caused by an arsonist at large in this close-knit Vermont community, and the secret Sue learns about her father after discovering his Civil War diary. This is an intriguing novel, particularly noteworthy for the ambiguous relationship between the sisters. An afterword explains that the characters and situations were taken from real life. For historical fiction lovers.

C.P.S.

Hermes, Patricia
On Winter's Wind

Little, Brown. 1995.   ISBN: 0-316-35978-5. 163 p.

It has been three years since Genevieve and her family have heard from her seafaring father. Although she is only eleven years old, Gen has become the family's sole means of support, both financially and emotionally. When an opportunity arises for Gen to turn in an escaped slave for the $100 bounty, which could mean the difference between survival and destitution, Gen must evaluate her feelings about slavery and an individual's responsibility to others in order to make the right decision. Gen is an interesting, independent, and strong female character at odds with the society of her time. Well written and enjoyable.

C.P.S.

McKissack, Patricia
Run Away Home

Scholastic. 1997.   ISBN: 0-590-46751-4. 160 p.

It is 1886 in Alabama, and eleven-year-old Sarah Jane witnesses a boy escaping from a train carrying Apache prisoners to a reservation in the Southwest. Instead of reporting his escape, Sarah decides that he should be given the same chance as the slaves who escaped to Canada on the Underground Railroad during the Civil War. Her family takes in the ailing Apache boy, and what Sarah initially sees as an unwelcome intrusion into her life soon becomes a riveting demonstration of the terrible discriminatory practices carried out against Native Americans and African Americans by whites. McKissack captures this bad time in American history in a way that will hold the attention of middle readers to the very last page.

B.D.V.

Walter Dean Myers has written a powerful book about an African American family that spans five generations. The story begins in 1753 and moves all the way to the present, showing one family's neverending struggle, over more than 200 years, for the freedom they deserve. Myer's excellent saga is filled with adventure and heroism, perfect for depicting slavery in the United States.

Myers, Walter Dean
The Glory Field

Scholastic. 1994.   ISBN: 0-590-45897-3. 375 p.

The shackles that held eleven-year-old Muhammad Bilal as the slave ship took him from Africa to South Carolina in 1753 are a focal point in a novel that follows five generations of an African American family over a 250-year period. From thirteen-year-old Lizzie, who stole away from working in the field to find freedom; to Tommy, who was invited to integrate a college during the civil rights movement; and Malcolm, who is on his way to a big Lewis family reunion at the Glory Field in 1994, the rich history of the Lewis family is told in five gripping episodes. Readers who stick with this lengthy saga will be richly rewarded.

L.W.

Paterson, Katherine
Lyddie

Puffin Books. 1991.   ISBN: 0-14-034981-2. 182 p.

After being abandoned by their father and hired out by their mother, Lyddie and Charles learn to make their way alone. Young girls are being hired as factory workers in the mills of Lowell, Massachusetts, and Lyddie is determined to earn enough money to buy back the family farm and reunite what is left of her family. She works six days a week, from dawn to dusk, running weaving looms in a dark factory where the air is filled with lint. When the poor working conditions begin to affect the girls' health, Lyddie must make a choice about speaking up for better working conditions and risk losing her job. Lyddie is an admirable heroine, and older readers will hope that she can succeed.

L.W.

Gary Paulsen, the popular author who is well loved for his adventure stories, takes a turn in historical fiction with the next two unforgettable books about the horrors of slavery. The character of Sarny comes to life as she relates her experiences and her commitment to survival.

Paulsen, Gary
Nightjohn

Delacorte Press. 1993.   ISBN: 0-385-30838-8. 92 p.

Sarny is a twelve-year-old slave owned by the Waller family. In her short life she's learned many things about surviving; what she hasn't learned, and longs to, is how to read. When an escaped slave is brought to the plantation, shackled and bleeding, Sarny seizes the opportunity to exchange a chaw of tobacco for her ABCs. Although she knows that the penalty for reading is dismemberment, she is determined to continue her lessons, realizing that the only hope she has lies in educating herself. This book's format, with its large font size and plenty of white space, will attract the third-grade reader; however, its descriptions of the horrifying conditions in which slaves lived may be more suitable for the older child. A haunting reading experience.

Series/Sequels: *Nightjohn*; *Sarny: A Life Remembered*

C.P.S.

Paulsen, Gary
Sarny: A Life Remembered

Delacorte Press. 1997.   ISBN: 0-385-32195-3. 180 p.

It is 1930 and Sarny, the slave girl who learned to read in *Nightjohn*, is now ninety-four years old and writing her own memoirs. Sarny recounts her life from the time Nightjohn left, up until 1930, as she looks back on her long life. Sarny's life is filled with trials and excitement as she travels to New Orleans to find her children who were sold into slavery. Life begins again when Sarny meets and becomes friends with Miss Laura. She finds her children, remarries, and goes on to set up schools for blacks throughout Texas. Paulsen has given his readers the gift of knowing what becomes of Sarny in this rich sequel. Older readers won't be disappointed.

Series/Sequels: *Nightjohn*; *Sarny: A Life Remembered*

B.D.V.

Polacco, Patricia
⬛PB Pink and Say

Philomel. 1994.   ISBN: 0-399-22671-0. Unpaged.

Two fifteen-year-old Union soldiers, one white and one black, meet during the war and form a strong, if brief, friendship. When Sheldon Russell Curtis is wounded while deserting, he is rescued by Pinkus Ayles and taken home to be nursed by Pink's mother, Moe Moe Bay. Their few days of happiness away from the battlefield are brutally shattered when Moe Moe Bay is murdered by Confederate soldiers and the boys are sent to the infamous Andersonville Prison, where one dies and one barely survives. A sobering introduction to the Civil War, this picture book for older children is based on a true story.

C.P.S.

Reeder, Carolyn
Across the Lines

Atheneum Books for Young Readers. 1997.   ISBN: 0-689-81133-0. 220 p.

The year is 1864, and Edward, the son of a white plantation owner, is separated from Simon, his longtime companion, who is black. The boys have grown up together and become best friends, but Simon will always be a house servant, the property of Edward's family, until he escapes to freedom with the arrival of the Union army. Reeder's story captures the reality of the Civil War through the eyes of two boys on opposite sides of the battle. Even though neither boy is directly in the line of fire, the book captures the cruelty and destruction that were prevalent throughout the war and beyond. This is a great read for middle and older readers and history buffs.

B.D.V.

Rees, Douglas
Lightning Time: A Novel

DK Publishing. 1997.   ISBN: 0-7894-2458-4. 166 p.

Fourteen-year-old Theodore Worth knew that slavery was dividing the country, but it wasn't until the abolitionist, John Brown, hid from the police in his home that he understood what his role in the battle would be. Two years later, in 1859, Theo ran away from his family to join up with Brown and his men, the Invisibles, and fight the army over slavery. Rees has shown what was going on in the United States before the Civil War began. He captures the feelings over the slavery issue and presents this tension, which led to violence and eventually war, through Theo's eyes, as he learns to question right and wrong. Middle and older readers will find an action-packed story that is rich in historical information.

B.D.V.

Rosen, Michael J.; Aminah Brenda Lynn Robinson, illus.
PB A School for Pompey Walker

Harcourt Brace Children's Books. 1995.   ISBN: 0-15-200114-X. Unpaged.

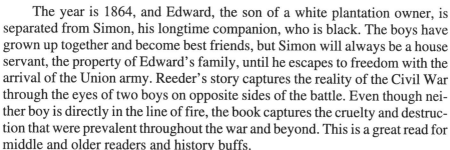

Pompey Walker, formerly Pompey Bibb, was a ninety-year-old African-American and former slave, who told his tale of hardship and courage to the children at the school that was being named in his honor, on September 8, 1923. Pompey told how he and Jeremiah Walker worked together to get Pompey sold into slavery, where he would escape only to be resold, so that they could earn money to build a school for black children. Rosen's story is a composite of several tales about this insufferable time in American history. This vivid portrayal, with hard-hitting illustrations, works well with a class or when read individually.

Awards: ALA Notable Books for Children, 1996

B.D.V.

Wisler, C. Clifton
Redcap

Dutton. 1991.   ISBN: 0-525-67337-7. 160 p.

Although he is only thirteen in 1862, Ransom Powell has already lost close friends in the Civil War. Despite being barely four feet tall, Ranse manages to convince a captain in the Union army to let him join as a drummer. His career is shortlived, as he is soon captured by Confederate troops and sent to the infamous Andersonville Prison. There Ranse manages to survive horrific living conditions while at the same time keeping his pledge to the Union forces by refusing to sign a parole that would free him. This book is based on the true-life experiences of a private in the Civil War and is a thoughtful portrait of one young boy's struggle to live decently in an indecent situation.

C.P.S.

Twentieth Century

As we all begin the twenty-first century, we can look back on the twentieth century and reflect on the many events that set the course for our future. The automobile was invented during the first decade of the century, giving Americans new freedom to see and travel through the country. There were the Depression and the Dust Storms of the 1930s, both of which had a heavy impact on the economic strength of the country.

World Wars I and II took the country, and the rest of the world, by storm, changing the way the United States looked at itself and at other countries around the world. The Americans witnessed the horrors inflicted on the Jewish people during the Holocaust, and fought to liberate them, treating them more like neighbors than foreigners involved in a hideous situation, thousands of miles away. Freedom for everyone became an issue worth fighting for. Gradually, it became unacceptable to discriminate because of race, religion, heritage, or sex. African Americans, after 200 years of discrimination, were finally being recognized and treated as equal citizens. Native Americans and Japanese Americans were also receiving the apologies they deserved and the respect due them as equals. Many mistakes were made in this century, but many advances and understandings were also achieved because of the strength of the American people. Many of these memorable times are brought to life in the following books, with stories about amazing young people who helped to change the direction of the country, most often for the better.

Burandt, Harriet, and Shelley Dale
Tales from the Homeplace: Adventures from a Texas Farm Girl

Henry Holt. 1997.   ISBN: 0-8050-5075-2. 154 p.

Twelve-year-old Irene is the main character in nine stories about life on a Texas farm in the 1930s. The stories are based on Burandt's memories of her sometimes difficult, often funny, and always lively life as she grew up on the farm in Texas. Her stories are built around Irene and her six younger brothers and sisters. They encounter such things as a hungry panther looking for dinner, the job of getting rid of the mice in the barn, and the young mother from another farm who shows up with unexplained bruises all over her body that are somehow linked to her husband. Each story gives middle readers a real sense of farm life in the 1930s.

B.D.V.

Cameron, Ann
The Secret Life of Amanda K. Woods

Farrar, Straus & Giroux. 1998.   ISBN: 0-374-36702-7. 201 p.

Amanda Wood's best friend Lyle moved to Montana, and eleven-year-old Amanda was left to face fifth grade alone, in the suburbs of Wisconsin during the 1950s. Amanda's mother described her as "average," compared to her beautiful big sister Margaret, but Amanda knew that on the inside she was much more. Then Amanda changed her name to "Amanda K. Woods" for emphasis and distinction. She found a new friend named Pam, and discovered that there really was an exciting person named Amanda who was much more than average. Cameron's skillful way of describing the ups and downs of family life is right on target with Amanda. Readers with siblings will relate to this well-developed character who grows up in the 1950s.

B.D.V.

Curtis, Christopher Paul
The Watsons Go to Birmingham—1963

Delacorte Press. 1995.   ISBN: 0-385-32175-9. 210 p.

Beset by money problems and concerns for their son Byron's increasingly rebellious behavior, the "Weird Watsons" of Flint, Michigan, decide to spend some time in Alabama with Grandma Sands, hopeful that the slower pace of the South will be a positive influence on the entire family. Younger brother Kenny's account of his family's experiences is both a side-splittingly funny and a terribly sad tale of what is was like to grow up African American in the pre-civil rights 1960s. Byron's run-in with a car's rearview mirror will have children (and adults) rolling on the floor. A joy for all readers.

Awards: Newbery Medal Honor Book, 1996; ALA Notable Books for Children, 1996

C.P.S.

John D. Fitzgerald, the author of the thoroughly delightful Great Brain series, died in 1988 after completing seven Great Brain books. Children are just as delighted with these books today as they were when Fitzgerald first began them in 1967. In honor of Fitzgerald, his editor pulled together this eighth and final book from some chapters that Fitzgerald wrote before he died. Even though Fitzgerald wasn't here for the completion, *The Great Brain Is Back* is just as zany and delightful as the other seven. This truly is a real find and well worth reading.

Fitzgerald, John; Diane DeGroat, illus.
The Great Brain Is Back

Dial Books for Young Readers. 1995.   ISBN: 0-8037-1346-0. 120 p.

Tom Fitzgerald, the Great Brain, is back, leading his brother J.D. and all the other kids in Adenville, Utah, in more schemes and adventures. Tom is thirteen, and Polly Reagan has cast a spell on him, but he still has time to figure out how to get more of his favorite thing—money. It has been twenty years since the last Great Brain book, but this eighth and final one still has the power to charm today's children.

Series/Sequels: The Great Brain Series: *The Great Brain*; *More Adventures of the Great Brain*; *Me and My Little Brain*; *The Great Brain at the Academy*; *The Great Brain Reforms*; *Return of the Great Brain*; *The Great Brain Does It Again*; *The Great Brain Is Back*

L.W.

Freeman, Suzanne
The Cuckoo's Child

Greenwillow Books. 1996.   ISBN: 0-688-14290-7. 249 p.

It is 1962, and Mia is miserable because she and her family have been living in Beirut for three years, where her father is teaching. She knows she is missing out on the normal life of a young person in America, where children eat Sloppy Joes, have barbecues, and go to the movies. Mia just wants to return to America and be normal. When Mia's parents set sail for Greece and never return, Mia does return to the States, only to face a new set of problems. This is a moving story about separation, loss, and adjustment in a new environment during the 1960s. Older readers will be drawn to this tale and held to the exciting conclusion.

Awards: ALA Best Books for Young Adults, 1997

B.D.V.

Griffin, Adele
Rainy Season

Houghton Mifflin. 1996.   IISBN: 0-395-81181-3. 200 p.

It is 1977, and twelve-year-old Lane is living in Panama. President Carter has just announced plans to return the Canal to local authority, and the social uneasiness caused by this decision is mirrored in Lane's unsettled feelings about her family and friends. To make matters worse, her older brother's behavior has become increasingly erratic since an automobile accident. This novel covers one day in Lane's life as she struggles to hold things together. Though well written, a host of unsympathetic characters and an unfamiliar setting might restrict its appeal to truly avid readers.

C.P.S.

Hall, Donald; Barry Moser, illus.
`PB` When Willard Met Babe Ruth

Browndeer Press. 1996.   ISBN: 0-15-200273-1. 41 p.

Who would have imagined that the driver who slid into the ditch on Willard's farm would be his baseball hero, Babe Ruth? He gives Willard a glove that becomes Willard's most prized possession. The next year, in 1918, when Willard and his father see Babe Ruth play at Fenway Park, the famous player remembers Willard and gives him a baseball. As the years go by, Willard notes every home run Babe Ruth ever makes. In 1935, Willard has a daughter named Ruth (after his hero), and they meet him one more time. Babe Ruth comes to life in this richly illustrated story.

L.W.

Hausman, Gerald
Doctor Moledinky's Castle: A Hometown Tale

Simon & Schuster Books for Young Readers. 1995.   ISBN: 0-689-80019-3. 151 p.

Once upon a time there was a small town, like any other small town, but different. Here, sober men danced down the streets with watermelons in their arms and farmers tickled their chickens' tummies before bringing down the axe. In fourteen magical, mysterious chapters, many of which can be read on their own, Andy describes the weird and funny goings-on in the Berkeley Bend of the 1950s, particularly the adventures he shares with his best friend, Pauley Barlow. A hilarious, thoroughly entertaining book for the discriminating reader.

C.P.S.

Karen Hesse has written two excellent books, one of which was the 1998 Newbery Medal winner, on different events that happened to people who were struggling to make—and keep—a place for themselves in the twentieth-century United States. Her writing captures the real struggles these people faced and the courage they exhibited to achieve their American dream.

Hesse, Karen
Letters from Rifka

Henry Holt. 1992.   ISBN: 0-8050-1964-2. 148 p.

In a series of diary entries written to her cousin Tovah, twelve-year-old Rifka relates her family's escape from Russia in 1919 and their perilous journey to America. Rifka is separated from her family after contracting ringworm, which delays her entry into the United States, and must wait alone in Belgium until she is well. This novel is based on the experiences of the author's great-aunt and is an inspiring portrait of both one family's struggle against religious persecution and a young girl's courage. A strong entry into the growing list of books about immigration.

C.P.S.

Hesse, Karen
Out of the Dust

Scholastic. 1997.   ISBN: 0-590-36080-9. 227 p.

Billie Jo tells the story of her life in the Oklahoma dust bowl during the Great Depression, through a series of poems. It would seem that she doesn't have much to be happy about: her mother died just when Billie Jo needed her most; because her father caused the accident that killed her mother, he is too distraught to help Billie Jo; the dust blows constantly and seeps into every crevice of their lives; and the crops won't grow. Somehow, Billie Jo still gathers hope from small, everyday happenings. This spare, exquisitely written novel conveys the emotions of the land, the time, and the heart.

Awards: Newbery Medal Book, 1998; ALA Notable Books for Children, 1998; ALA Best Books for Young Adults, 1998

L.W.

6

Hest, Amy; Sonja Lamut, illus.
The Private Notebooks of Katie Roberts, Age 11

Candlewick Press. 1995.   ISBN: 1-56402-474-1. 75 p.

When Katie Roberts was seven, her father was killed in World War II. Now she is eleven and her whole life is going to change. Her mother is marrying Sam Gold, and they are moving from New York City to Sam's ranch in Texas. Katie is sure she will hate Texas, that no one there will be Jewish, and that she won't have any friends. Katie uses the red leather notebook her friend Mrs. Leitstein gave her to keep a diary, draw pictures, and write letters. These first-person materials form the book in this sequel to *Love You, Soldier*.

Series/Sequels: *Love You, Soldier*; *The Private Notebooks of Katie Roberts, Age 11*

L.W.

Hill, Anthony; Mark Sofilas, illus.
PB The Burnt Stick

Houghton Mifflin. 1995.   ISBN: 0-395-73974-8. 53 p.

John Jagamarra, a character with part-aborigine and part-white heritage, is taken from his aborigine tribe when he is five, to be raised in a white missionary school to learn the ways of white society. Although this particular story is fictional, it was actually the practice of the Australians until 1960, when working with children of mixed parentage. It is an important picture book for older readers that shouldn't be missed. It makes an excellent read-aloud, taking the audience to the heart of ignorance, racism, and misunderstanding. Its presentation is thought-provoking and nonthreatening, setting the stage for lively classroom discussion.

B.D.V.

Hyatt, Patricia Rusch
Coast to Coast with Alice

Carolrhoda Books. 1995.   ISBN: 0-87614-789. 72 p.

In 1909, automobiles were brand new, and Alice Ramsey was going to be the first woman to drive one across the United States. One of Alice's passengers is sixteen-year-old Minna Jahns. She keeps a journal about all the unusual and exciting things that happen on the trip. Photographs help to tell the true story of how four women crossed the country—3,800 miles—in only fifty-nine days. This fictionalized account of an historical event is sure to delight the adventurer in each reader.

L.W.

Johnston, Julie
Hero of Lesser Causes

Little, Brown. 1992.   ISBN: 0-316-46988-2. 194 p.

Keely and her brother Patrick, who are twelve and thirteen respectively, are the best of friends. They thrive on dares, from wading in a pond infested with leeches to crossing a river on a high, narrow plank. Everything changes when Patrick becomes ill with polio and is paralyzed. The year is 1946, and polio is a dreaded disease.

Keely's greatest challenge comes as she does everything possible to try to interest her depressed and despondent brother in anything. Patrick's bitter despair and Keely's determination to help him heal provide a spirited story of siblings facing nearly impossible challenges.

L.W.

Kinsey-Warnock, Natalie
As Long as There Are Mountains

Cobblehill Books. 1997.   ISBN: 0-525-65236-1. 139 p.

It is 1956, and thirteen-year-old Iris feels that life couldn't be better. She loves the farm that her family owns in Vermont, and hopes to inherit it when she grows up. Things change for the worse, though, when the family's barn burns down, and Iris' father is permanently injured in a bad accident. Can Iris and her family weather the hardships when money is so tight, or will they have to sell the farm and move to the city to find work? This is a strong story about farm life, and about the challenges of personal growth and maturity that Iris must face. Middle and older readers will be drawn to this rich novel about family life in the 1950s.

B.D.V.

Levin, Betty
Fire in the Wind

Greenwillow Books. 1995.   ISBN: 0-688-14299-0. 137 p.

Based on a true story about wildfires that devastated many communities and woodlands in Maine in 1947, this is the tale of how a disaster brought a family together. Meg's family was still mourning the death of her cousin Champ in World War II, and it took the fire to help everyone recognize the strength of Orin, his younger brother. Orin became the town hero after saving the lives of his cousins, Meg and Paul. Although this story moves slowly, readers who complete the book will feel great satisfaction when the underdog wins.

L.W.

Little, Jean
His Banner over Me

Viking. 1995.   ISBN: 0-670-85664-9. 205 p.

Flora (Gorrie) Gauld is the child of missionaries in Taiwan during the early 1900s. When she is five years old, Gorrie; her sister Gretta, who is seven; her brother William, who is four; and baby Dorothy are taken to live with their relatives in Canada so they can go to school. At the age of sixteen, Flora begins medical school and becomes a doctor. Jean Little's novel is based on the life of her mother, Flora Gauld Little, whose life bridged two worlds and two families from Taiwan to Canada.

L.W.

Mooney, Bel
The Voices of Silence

Delacorte Press. 1997.   ISBN: 0-385-32326-3. 180 p.

Caught up in the political turmoil of the Ceausescu dictatorship in Romania, thirteen-year-old Flora Popescu watches with increasing alarm as her world falls apart, with her estrangement from friend Alys and her parents' secretive behavior. Feeling desperately lonely, she rashly confides in Daniel Ghiban, a popular new student in her school, describing an overheard conversation in which her parents plot to escape the country. Despite an unfamiliar setting, readers will find Flora's predicament interesting and a thought-provoking introduction to recent political events in Eastern Europe.

C.P.S.

Michael Morpurgo, well known for his historical fiction and particularly tales about the struggles of the Jewish people in World War II, takes a look at different times in these two books—certainly material for discussion!

Morpurgo, Michael
The War of Jenkins Ear

Philomel. 1995.   ISBN: 0-399-22735-0. 171 p.

It is 1952 at an English boys' boarding school. The strange new boy, Christopher, isn't like the other boys. Can he really be Jesus, as he claims? Relationships among people, both good and evil, are explored in this complex novel, which leaves the reader with many questions.

Awards: ALA Best Books for Young Adults, 1996

L.W.

Morpurgo, Michael; François Place, illus.
The Wreck of the Zanzibar

Viking. 1995.   ISBN: 0-670-86360-2. 69 p.

Great-Aunt Laura was one hundred years old when she died and left a package for each member of the family. Her great-nephew, Michael, received a handmade book, *The Diary of Laura Perryman*. Laura's story is a fascinating tale of a young girl whose dream is to join her father and brother when they row out to salvage ships wrecked at sea. But girls don't row in gigs. Meanwhile, she writes about her life, her Granny May, a sea turtle she rescues, and the storms that wreck ships. Finally her wish comes true. The diary, interspersed with watercolors, tells a unique and memorable story that links two generations.

L.W.

O'Leary, Patsy Baker
With Wings as Eagles

Houghton Mifflin. 1997.   ISBN: 0-395-70557-6. 262 p.

When his father is released from prison for moonshining, twelve-year-old Bubba is resentful of this new authority at home. Not only does Jed expect obedience, he wants Bubba to distance himself from Israel, the black man who has become his surrogate father. When Bubba accidentally discovers that Israel may have been responsible for his father's unjust imprisonment, he becomes confused and rebellious. The threat of losing the family farm causes Jed to reevaluate his feelings for these two men. This beautiful novel, set in North Carolina in the 1930s, is an engrossing look at prejudice and forgiveness. Highly recommended.

C.P.S.

Oughton, Jerrie
6-8 **Music from a Place Called Half Moon**

Houghton Mifflin. 1995.   ISBN: 0-395-70737-4. 160 p.

The year is 1956, and tension is running high in Half Moon, North Carolina, as strong feelings of prejudice against the Native Americans begin to escalate. During this heated time, thirteen-year-old Edie Jo becomes friends with Cherokee Fish, a sensitive Native American boy at school. They share their interests in writing and music until violence and, ultimately, tragedy end their friendship. This is a riveting account of what happens when discrimination and hatred take control of people's lives. This excellent story is for older, more experienced readers because of some violence and strong language.

Awards: Children's Book Award, the Child Study Children's Book Committee at Bank Street College, 1995

B.D.V.

Partridge, Elizabeth
Clara and the Hoo Doo Man

Dutton Children's Books. 1996.   ISBN: 0-525-45403-9. 168 p.

Clara breaks a crock used for storing sausage in the winter. Money is scarce for Clara's family in 1900, so she and her sister, Bessie, search for plants to sell to the barterman so they can replace the much-needed crock. A fierce storm erupts while they are looking, and when they finally return home, Bessie is near death with a high fever. Their own doctor is away and the white doctor in town is no help at all. As a last resort, Clara turns to the herbal healer, the man who lives at the top of the mountain and is known to all as the evil hoo doo man. This is a page-turning adventure mixed with some remarkable information about herbs, for middle readers.

B.D.V.

The following book by Richard Peck received the 1999 Newbery Honor Award. He has put together a series of short stories that, when read together, paint a rich picture of country life during the Depression, and the love and understanding that develop between a grandmother and her grandchildren.

Peck, Richard
A Long Way from Chicago

Dial Books for Young Readers. 1998   ISBN: 0-8037-2290-7. 148 p.

Joey was only nine years old, and his sister Mary Alice just seven, when Joey began recounting the hilarious summers they would spend with their grandmother in Illinois throughout the Depression. Every year the two children would leave the big city and travel by train to the country where, surprisingly, life turned out to be anything but slow and quiet. As the years passed, the children came to love and admire the grandmother who had a larger than life personality and could take on any challenge, no matter how outrageous or unbelievable. Peck's ability to tell a whopper of a tale has never been better than in these short stories that build to present an amazing grandmother. Definitely an award winner for Peck.

Awards: Newbery Award Honor Book, 1999

B.D.V.

Porter, Tracey
Treasures in the Dust

Joanna Cotler Books. 1997. ISBN: 0-06-027563-4. 148 p.

Annie and Violet, two eleven-year-olds who have been best friends on neighboring farms in Oklahoma, tell their stories in alternating chapters about how they survived the dust storms and the Depression that wreaked havoc on their lives during the 1930s. Annie's family remained in Oklahoma to fight the drought and dust that withered and suffocated their farm; Violet's family went to California to battle the poverty and discrimination that plagued the migrant workers. Porter's story about this destitute period in American history is so lifelike and dramatic that middle readers will almost feel the dust on the pages while reading this page-turner!

B.D.V.

Rael, Elsa Okon; Marjorie Priceman, illus.
What Zeesie Saw on Delancey Street

Simon & Schuster Books for Young Readers. 1996. ISBN: 0-689-80549-7. Unpaged.

It is the early 1900s, and Zeesie has her seventh birthday to celebrate. Now that she is grown up, she can attend a "package party" with her Mama and Papa. Everyone attending the party brings a package to be auctioned off to raise money for other immigrants coming to America. Zeesie could make a bid on any package with her new dollar, but what is happening behind the closed doors in the money room? Zeesie learns about the joys of giving and receiving in this splendid picture book for older readers. Along with Priceman's illustrations, it provides an excellent starting point for a discussion on character traits.

Awards: ALA Notable Books for Children, 1997

B.D.V.

Slepian, Jan
Pinocchio's Sister

Philomel. 1995. ISBN: 0-399-22811-X. 122 p.

It is 1928, and vaudeville is still a major form of entertainment. Ten-year-old Martha travels on the vaudeville circuit with her father, but she is becoming increasingly anxious and unhappy. Martha's mother is dead, her stepmother runs off with a juggler, and Martha's father has been withdrawn and introspective ever since. He is only interested in his beautiful Iris, the wooden dummy in his vaudeville act, and he totally neglects his real daughter. Here is a chilling but memorable tale about the effects of parental neglect and abuse on a child. This dark, powerful story will speak to a special group of sensitive middle readers.

B.D.V.

Sterling, Shirley
My Name Is Seepeetza

Douglas & McIntyre. 1997.   ISBN: 0-88899-290-4. 126 p.

Living on Joyaska Ranch with her parents, brothers, sisters, and pets is heaven to Seepeetza. But when she is six years old, she is driven to the town of Kalamak in British Columbia to spend years at an Indian residential school. There the nuns call her Martha, cut her hair, and forbid her to "talk Indian." She is selected to be a dancer, representing the school, but the dancing is Irish, not Indian. The children are treated with great cruelty by the sisters, and only thoughts of going home at Christmas and during the summer make life bearable for Seepeetza. This novel is based on the author's own experiences during the 1950s.

L.W.

Mildred Taylor is currently one of the most respected authors writing children's books today. Her Logan Family series spans the past twenty-five years in American history, and demonstrates well the racism that is still burning a hole in so many people's hearts across the country. Her books not only give her readers exciting and memorable stories, but also teach them about the sad realities that have existed and still exist today for African Americans. The next two books are part of her insightful series.

Taylor, Mildred D.
The Road to Memphis

Dial Books for Young Readers. 1990.   ISBN: 803703406. 290 p.

Even though the world is caught up in the war in Europe and the Pacific, Cassie Logan is much more concerned with trouble at home in Mississippi in the 1940s. Racism and violence have become a big part of everyday life for the Logan family and their friends. Although this novel stands alone, it will certainly be well received by those who met Cassie Logan in *Roll of Thunder, Hear My Cry*, when she was a young girl first experiencing the sting of racism in the South. Now the characters are older and still dealing with the biting cruelties of racism. The story is powerful and will be remembered by every reader long after it is finished.

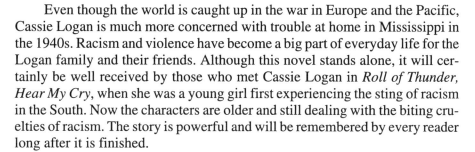

Awards: Coretta Scott King Award, 1990; George C. Stone Center Award, 1990

Series/Sequels: Logan Family Series: *Song of the Trees*; *Roll of Thunder, Hear My Cry*; *Let the Circle Be Unbroken*; *The Friendship*; *The Road to Memphis*; *Mississippi Bridge*; *The Well: David's Story*

L.W.

Taylor, Mildred D.
The Well: David's Story

Dial Books for Young Readers. 1995.   ISBN: 0-803-721802-0. 92 p.

When a severe drought leaves most of their rural Mississippi farming community without water, the Logans, a respected black landholding family, have enough water to share with others. The idea of being beholden to "niggers" doesn't sit well with Charlie Simms, an ignorant white youth whose rage in the face of his helplessness and the Logans' generosity results in his ruining the well. This novella is powerful, frightening, and beautifully written; many readers, both young and old alike, will have difficulty controlling their indignation and anger in the face of such stupidity and injustice.

Awards: ALA Notable Books for Children, 1996

Series/Sequels: Logan Family Series: *Song of the Trees*; *Roll of Thunder, Hear My Cry*; *Let the Circle Be Unbroken*; *The Friendship*; *The Road to Memphis*; *Mississippi Bridge*; *The Well: David's Story*

C.P.S.

Temple, Frances
Tonight, by Sea

Orchard. 1995.   ISBN: 0-06-440670-9 (pbk). 152 p.

It is 1986, and life in Haiti is becoming more treacherous for Paulie and her family. The social system in Haiti is changing. There isn't enough food, trees are disappearing as people cut them down to build boats with, and many villagers have already fled the country. The trouble escalates when the *macoutes*, the terrorist army within the Haitian military organized to attack fellow Haitians, begin terrorizing Paulie's family and neighbors. Paulie's family flees too, but will they be safe on their journey, and then accepted in the United States? This moving, sometimes graphic account captures the terror facing immigrants. A timely historical novel for older readers.

Awards: Americas Award for Children's and Young Adult Literature, 1995

B.D.V.

Ronder Thomas Young has a real understanding of the good times, and of the hardships that took place in the cities of this country during the past century. Both of these stories give readers a lot to reflect on about the struggles of city life.

Young, Ronder Thomas
Learning by Heart

Houghton Mifflin. 1993.   ISBN: 0-395-65369-X. 172 p.

When Rachel is ten, her life changes dramatically when her family moves from the tiny apartment behind her parents' grocery store to a real house in a new neighborhood. Because her mother is pregnant and needs help, the family hires Isabella Harris, a very wise, young black woman. Rachel's eyes are opened to very different kinds of people, and with Isabella's guidance she learns understanding and acceptance. Rachel is particularly fascinated by the confidence and self-assurance displayed by Callie Thompson, the only black girl in Rachel's all-white school. This tender story has great depth and presents thoughtful insights into growing up in a small southern town in the 1960s.

L.W.

Young, Ronder Thomas
Moving Mama to Town

Orchard. 1997.   ISBN: 0-531-33025-7. 219 p.

Big Kenny had lots of advice, but he showed his true colors when he deserted his family. Freddy James Johnson is thirteen and is suddenly the man of the family. He moves his mama and his little brother, Kenneth Lee, from their farm to an apartment in the town that is run by Miss Precious Dolittle. With his job at Fenton's Fine Establishment, he thinks they can make ends meet. While reading this novel, set in 1947, mature readers will root for Freddy as he faces many challenges.

L.W.

World War II

Borden, Louise; Michael Forman, illus.
PB **The Little Ships: The Heroic Rescue at Dunkirk in World War II**

Margaret K. McElderry. 1997.   ISBN: 0-689-80827-5. Unpaged.

In May of 1940, half a million British and French soldiers were trapped by the Nazis. The only escape was by sea. In this fictionalized account of the rescue at Dunkirk, a young girl and her father take their fishing boat, *Lucy*, across the English Channel along with hundreds of other little boats, to rescue the trapped soldiers. Along with the soldiers, she also rescues a dog, Smoky Joe. This dramatic, true story of the rescue of 338,000 men is a fine example of a picture book for older readers. As the little ships and their passengers face the perilous sea and enemy planes, the reader is certain to be enthralled with this historical tale.

L.W.

Bunting, Eve
Spying on Miss Muller

Clarion Books. 1995.   ISBN: 0-395-69172-9. 179 p.

Thirteen-year-old Jessie is attending Alveara Boarding School in Belfast, Ireland, in 1939, at the beginning of World War II. Jessie and her friends have always liked and admired their friendly and attractive German teacher, Miss Muller, but then Jessie sees Miss Muller go up to the roof in the middle of the night—the same night as the first air raid on Belfast by the Germans. Could Miss Muller, who is half German, be a Nazi spy who signaled the Nazi war planes from the roof of their school? Eve Bunting presents a gripping novel about the consequences of fear and hatred, which can be particularly dangerous during the difficult times of war.

B.D.V.

6

Giff, Patricia Reilly
Lily's Crossing

Delacorte Press. 1997.   ISBN: 0-385-32142-2. 180 p.

The year is 1944, and World War II is changing life for everyone. Lily's best friend, Margaret, must move away, and Lily's father has to go overseas and help in the war effort. Lily must spend the summer between fifth and sixth grade in the beach town of Rockaway with her grandmother. During the summer, a Hungarian refugee named Albert moves to Rockaway, where he and Lily form a strong and lasting friendship. It is through this friendship that Lily comes to understand the pain of war and the importance of honesty between friends. This powerful, award-winning story will be read and cherished by many middle-grade readers.

Awards: Newbery Medal Honor Book, 1998; ALA Notable Books for Children, 1998

B.D.V.

Mary Downing Hahn has a big following because her many books speak directly to young people today, even though many of the characters in her stories are from the past. The following two books, which take place during the 1940s, discuss some pertinent issues that were current at that time, and that persist for many families today.

Hahn, Mary Downing
Stepping on the Cracks

Clarion Books. 1991.   ISBN: 0-395-58507-4. 216 p.

Margaret and Elizabeth are entering the sixth grade this year, and they both hope that Gordy Smith, the town bully, won't be tormenting them in school. Gordy, like both of the girls, has a brother who is away at war, for the year is 1944 and the United States is engaged in World War II. Gordy is being even more abusive than ever, though, so the girls begin to spy on him to find out what is happening. Margaret and Elizabeth discover why Gordy is causing so much trouble, but they also learn that there is more than one way to look at war. Hahn presents the side of choosing not to fight in war, and the emotions that surface and repercussions that affect everyone involved. This is an excellent, discussable story for older readers. The character of Gordy continues in Hahn's book, *Following My Own Footsteps*.

Awards: ALA Notable Books for Children, 1991

B.D.V.

Hahn, Mary Downing
Following My Own Footsteps

Clarion Books. 1996.   ISBN: 0-395-76477-7. 186 p.

It is 1945 when Gordy's mother finally leaves her alcoholic husband. Gordy has mixed feelings of both relief and apprehension when his mother makes the decision. While he will no longer be subjected to physical and verbal abuse, he's worried about meeting his grandmother, with whom the family will now be staying. At first Gordy can't stand this humorless woman, but he gradually learns to appreciate the structure that she gives to his life. When his father comes to collect the family, Gordy realizes that his future is more secure with his stern, but loving, grandmother, with whom he has at last found a caring home. Gordy first appears in *Stepping on the Cracks*.

C.P.S.

Heneghan, James
Wish Me Luck

Farrar, Straus & Giroux. 1997.   ISBN: 0-374-38453-3. 195 p.

The war is going on, but there isn't enough action to satisfy twelve-year-old Jamie Monaghan and his friends. Other than the air raids, which send the family scurrying to the bomb shelter and make it necessary to carry a gas mask everywhere, there are no other signs of war. Jamie certainly doesn't want to be sent away to safety, but his parents decide that Liverpool is no longer safe and book passage for him on the *City of Benares*, a ship bound for Canada. Instead of sailing to safety, things go wrong and Jamie gets closer to the war than anyone ever imagined. This gripping novel is based on a true story.

L.W.

Howard, Ellen
A Different Kind of Courage

Atheneum Books for Young Readers. 1996.   ISBN: 0-689-80774-0. 170 p.

In June 1940, the German army is almost to Paris, and nearly all of France is occupied. Bertrand, his mother, and his little sister Leonie are fleeing Paris in hopes of finding safety in America. In another city in France, Zina and Lisa Sarach and their parents are living with other Russians in a camp. No one has enough to eat, and everyone is afraid of the German soldiers and planes. The parents must send their children ahead to America. Based on a true story of an American woman, Martha Sharp, who saved a group of French children. Through this strong story, the reader relives the fear and loneliness of the children.

L.W.

Lee, Milly; Yangsook Choi, illus.
PB Nim and the War Effort

Farrar, Straus & Giroux. 1997.   ISBN: 0-374-35523-1. Unpaged.

Nim's school is participating in a competition to collect newspapers for the war effort; through great diligence, Nim is ahead. When her closest competitor, Garland Stephenson, tells her that only a "real" American can win the contest, Nim turns to an unlikely source for help. This picture book focuses on a culture many children may not be too familiar with, and the information about the role Chinese Americans played on the homefront during World War II should be of interest and spark thoughtful discussion.

C.P.S.

Manley, Joan B.
She Flew No Flags

Houghton Mifflin. 1995.   ISBN: 0-395-71130-4. 269 p.

In 1944, ten-year-old Janet Baylor and her family are sailing from India, where her father has been a missionary doctor, back to the United States. Because the ship must pass through enemy waters, it must travel with no flag, lights, or radio, to avoid being torpedoed. Janet and her brothers explore the ship, finding intrigue and excitement. Who is the beautiful Ann Dobson, and why is the little Chinese boy, Lee, so secretive about his past? Joan Manley, whose parents were medical missionaries during the war, drew on her own experiences to create this unique historical adventure novel.

6

L.W.

Napoli, Donna Jo
6-8 Stones in Water

Dutton Children's Books. 1997.   ISBN: 0-525-45842-5. 209 p.

A childhood prank ends in disaster when Roberto and his friends are rounded up by German soldiers and sent to a forced labor camp in the Ukraine. Roberto and Samuele, called Enzo to hide his identity as a Jew, manage to stay together through wretched conditions until Enzo is beaten to death by prisoners intent on stealing his shoes. Roberto realizes that he has no control over his destiny and therefore nothing to lose by attempting to escape. His flight and struggle to survive on the long journey home make for exciting reading. Napoli conveys the horrors of World War II in restrained, elegant prose.

Awards: ALA Best Books for Young Adults, 1998

C.P.S.

Paulsen, Gary
The Cookcamp

Orchard. 1991.   ISBN: 0-531-05927-8. 115 p.

When the boy was five years old, his father was away fighting in the war and his mother took a job in a factory. He was sent far away to his grandmother, who worked as a cook for a crew of nine men building a road to Canada. The big men intrigued him, with their loud ways and huge appetites, and he became their mascot. He helped drive the huge Caterpillar tractor with Gustav and drove the noisy dump truck with Carl. The love of his grandmother and the men enveloped him and helped ease his homesickness. The reader will wish that this lyrical, heartwarming story could go on and on. Though very accessible for younger readers, the story has something for everyone.

L.W.

Rinaldi, Ann
Keep Smiling Through

Harcourt Brace. 1996.   ISBN: 0-15-200768-7. 188 p.

It is the 1940s, and ten-year-old Kay Hemmings wants to be a heroine like the people in the stories she hears every day on the radio. With the war going on, Kay wants to do her part for her country, do what's right, and please others. Her biggest problem at home is her stepmother, Amazing Grace, who is a selfish, spiteful woman. The war is foremost in everyone's mind, and the song "Keep Smiling Through" becomes Kay's motto as she struggles to grow up during a difficult time. Rinaldi, in her superior style, has brought another historical period to life with the strong character of Kay.

L.W.

Ross, Ramon Royal
Harper & Moon

Atheneum. 1993.   ISBN: 0-689-31803-0. 181 p.

Sometimes the most unusual friendships are the best ones. That's how it is with Harper, Moon, and Olinger. Harper is twelve, Moon is in his teens (no one knows his exact age), and Olinger is an aging storekeeper who lives alone in his cabin in the Blue Mountains. For one magic week, Harper and Moon stay with Olinger up at his mountain cabin. Then World War II begins, and Moon enlists as a soldier. Left on his own, Harper makes a terrible discovery that threatens his friendship with Moon and Olinger. This is a story of courage, mystery, friendship, and trust for middle-grade readers.

L.W.

Salisbury, Graham
Under the Blood-Red Sun

Delacorte Press. 1994.   ISBN: 0-385-32099-X. 246 p.

The time is 1941, and thirteen-year-old Tomi, born in Hawaii to first-generation Japanese immigrants, is fully aware of the dangers associated with being Japanese. How, then, to convince Grandpa Joji to give up his all-too-obvious pride in his native country? When Pearl Harbor is attacked, Tomi and his family soon discover the perils they face, as his father and grandfather are arrested and sent to a prison camp and old friends turn against them. This is a fine, balanced examination of the injustices committed by often well-meaning people against loyal United States citizens.

C.P.S.

Robert Westall, who died in 1993, was a British author who grew up during World War II. His notoriety and tremendous popularity, which spanned two continents, came from his novels about the harsh realities of World War II. His stories are riveting, gritty, and really catch the action of the military and the hardware. Here are two of his action-packed novels that were published in the United States during the 1990s. Sometimes the British colloquialisms slow down the reading, but encourage readers to stick with it because the stories are well worth some effort.

Westall, Robert
The Kingdom by the Sea

Farrar, Straus & Giroux. 1991.   ISBN: 0-374-34205-9. 175 p.

By 1942, air raids have become commonplace to Harry Baguely. That is, until the night a bomb hits his back yard, and Harry is the only one in his family to reach the bomb shelter. Convinced that his Dad, Mam, and sister Dulcie are dead, Harry sets off for the coast to fend for himself. Fortunately, he finds a loyal friend in Don, an abandoned dog. Even in wartime, a boy on his own attracts attention, so Harry keeps on the move. He meets both kind and wicked people as he travels up the coast. Mature themes are woven into this incredible tale of adventure.

L.W.

 6

Westall, Robert
Time of Fire

Scholastic. 1997.   ISBN: 0-590-47746-3. 172 p.

Sonny is walking home from school, thinking that life hasn't changed that much even though England is in the midst of World War II. His mind is changed forever, though, when a fighter plane drops a bomb on his town. Now Sonny must deal with a war that is literally fought in his own backyard. Westall brings the reality of war home by developing a strong character who must not only face the death of his loved ones, but also decide if his mother's killer should live or die. This is a powerful novel about World War II, war planes, and guns that will captivate older readers if they can overlook the sometimes heavy British dialect.

B.D.V.

The next story, by Virginia Euwer Wolff, actually takes place four years after the end of World War II, but the feelings generated because of the war are still alive for many.

Wolff, Virginia Euwer
Bat 6
Scholastic. 1998.   ISBN: 0-590-89799-3. 230 p.

The year is 1949; it is four years after World War II and the fiftieth anniversary of Bat 6, the legendary softball game that has been played for the past forty-nine years between the sixth-grade girls from the neighboring towns of Barlow Road and Bear Creek Ridge. Through the eyes of each of the members of the opposing teams, the stage is set for that fateful day when the fiftieth Bat 6 is played. This year, each team has one new member: Aki, who has just returned to town from a Japanese internment camp; and Shazam, whose father was killed at Pearl Harbor. The tension in Wolff's story escalates until the crashing conclusion, which will leave every middle- and upper-grade reader moved.

B.D.V.

Yep, Laurence
Hiroshima
Scholastic. 1995.   ISBN: 0-590-20832-2. 56 p.

The events leading up to the bombing of Hiroshima, the actual attack, and the devastating aftermath are eloquently and simply presented in this novel. Focusing on the crew aboard the *Enola Gay*, the plane that delivered the bomb, and on a group of schoolchildren in Hiroshima, the author presents a dispassionate yet moving account. The simplicity of the writing stands in an effective contrast to the horror of the event and the book is an important addition to the growing list of outstanding books for children about the war. Use for a short, restrained introduction to Hiroshima.

C.P.S.

The Holocaust and Holocaust Survivors

Hoestlandt, Jo; Johanna Kang, illus.
[PB] Star of Fear, Star of Hope
Walker. 1995.   ISBN: 0-8027-8373-2. 32 p.

It is 1942. Tomorrow Helen will be nine, and her best friend, Lydia, is spending the night. Just a few days earlier, Helen watched Lydia's mother sew a yellow star on Lydia's jacket. She explains to the girls that a new law requires every Jew to wear a star. That night, there seems to be danger all around. The next day, Helen and her parents watch as all the people with yellow stars are taken away by the police. Haunting illustrations combined with a powerful story provide an introduction to the Holocaust in this picture book for older readers.

Awards: ALA Notable Books for Children, 1996; Mildred L. Batchelder Honor Book, 1996; Sydney Taylor Book Award, 1995

L.W.

Morpurgo, Michael
Waiting for Anya

Viking. 1991.   ISBN: 0-670-83735-0. 172 p.

When twelve-year-old Jo accidentally falls asleep while tending the sheep, a female bear is spotted and killed by the townspeople. Overcome with guilt, Jo runs to the hills to be alone. There Jo finds a bear cub and a man he has never seen before. Jo follows the man back to Widow Horcada's farm and discovers that the man and the widow are hiding Jewish children and taking them to the freedom of Spain. Now Jo wants to help with the escapes, but when the Nazi soldiers move into town, this becomes a difficult act for Jo and for the rest of the town. Morpurgo's story is both a gripping page-turner and a compelling story about the struggles facing the Jews during World War II.

Awards: ALA Best Books for Young Adults, 1991

B.D.V.

Orlev, Uri. Translated from the Hebrew by Hillel Halkin
The Man from the Other Side

Houghton Mifflin. 1991.   ISBN: 0-395-53808-4. 186 p.

Warsaw during World War II was a prison for thousands of Jews, who were held captive and murdered in the Warsaw Ghetto. Fourteen-year-old Marek, who lived in Warsaw, saw a man in his church who was obviously not a Catholic. Marek approached the man and, ultimately, he and his grandparents hid the man, named Pan Jozek, who was an escaped Jew from the ghetto. When Pan Jozek wanted to return to the ghetto, though, and fight for freedom with his people, did Marek truly understand the bravery and self-respect of the Jews? Orlev's award-winning novel is based on a gripping true story of escape in the sewers of Warsaw. All upper-grade readers will be moved by this unforgettable account.

Awards: ALA Notable Books for Children, 1991; Mildred L. Batchelder Award, 1992; National Jewish Book Award, 1992

B.D.V.

Semel, Nava
Flying Lessons

Simon & Schuster Books for Young Readers. 1995.   ISBN: 0-689-80161-0. 119 p.

Hadara's small village in Israel has one of almost everything: one grocer, one doctor, one nurse, one shoemaker, and one child without a mother. That child is Hadara, who lives with her father, a citrus grower. Hadara dreams of flying. When Maurice Havivel, the shoemaker, tells her stories of the circus, Hadara decides that he is the person who can teach her to fly. She is very impatient to learn. Although she doesn't quite become the first Jewish trapeze artist in Israel, Hadara does learn a great deal about life and people. This lyrical translation of an Israeli novel tells a unique story of Holocaust survivors.

L.W.

Vos, Ida
Dancing on the Bridge of Avignon

Houghton Mifflin. 1995.   ISBN: 0-395-72039-7. 183 p.

Life for ten-year-old Rosa and her family has changed dramatically since the Nazi occupation of Holland began in World War II. Because Rosa is Jewish, she and her sister can no longer attend school. As time passes, the list of restrictions grows and more Jewish people are either sent to work camps or flee the country for safety. Tension builds to an unimaginable climax, as Vos shows the readers what happened to ordinary Jewish citizens during World War II. The book is an excellent, straightforward account of the damage prejudices can cause when they are taken to an extreme. Middle readers will be drawn to this expressive story.

Awards: Sydney Taylor Book Award, 1995

B.D.V.

Williams, Laura E.; A. Nancy Goldstein, illus.
Behind the Bedroom Wall

Milkweed Editions. 1996.   ISBN: 1-57131-606-X. 169 p.

The year is 1942, and thirteen-year-old Korinna is an active member of the local Nazi youth group in her German town. Korinna and her friends believe that Hitler is building a stronger Germany, and they want to help by reporting any German citizens who aren't working to get rid of the "Jewish problem" in their town. When Korinna finds out that her parents are hiding a Jewish family in her own home, she must decide if she should report her parents to the authorities for the good of her country. Williams's story is a thought-provoking look at the Holocaust from a different perspective, offering dynamic reading for middle readers.

Awards: Milkweed Prize for Children's Literature, 1996

B.D.V.

Short Stories

Isaacs, Anne; Lloyd Bloom, illus.
Treehouse Tales

Dutton Children's Books. 1997.   ISBN: 0-525-45611-2. 85 p.

Tom, his sister Emily, and their youngest brother Natty are three delightful characters who live with their parents on a farm in Pennsylvania. The time is the 1880s, but the adventures could be happening today, as each child narrates a different tale that is somehow connected to their treehouse. Tom, Emily, and Natty all have the spunk, initiative, and creativity that fill these stories with both humor and tenderness, as each character comes alive in his or her own story. Younger readers will identify with these stories and find themselves laughing out loud as the characters tell about their adventures. The historical setting rings true to the activities taking place at that time.

B.D.V.

Salisbury, Graham
Blue Skin of the Sea

Delacorte Press. 1992.   ISBN: 0-385-30596-6. 215 p.

Eleven stories, with the common thread of the sea, tell the story of Sonny Mendoza as he grows up in Hawaii between 1953 and 1966. His home in a Hawaiian fishing village is alive with family, friendship, and the ever-present unpredictability of the sea. The stories begin when Sonny is a young boy, playing with his cousin Keo, and follow him to the high school, which is inland and worlds away from the sea. The author, who grew up on Oahu and Hawaii, easily draws readers into the places he loves.

L.W.

Paperback Historical Fiction Series

Series: American Diaries

Author: Duey, Kathleen

Publisher: Aladdin Paperbacks

Informative pieces of American history are presented in each of these novels. The stories begin and end with consecutive pages from the female narrators' diaries. Even though only one day passes between each entry, the books offer lively accounts of the events occurring in the country during those memorable times.

Titles: 1. *Sarah Anne Hartford: Massachusetts, 1651*
2. *Emma Eileen Grove: Mississippi, 1865*
3. *Anisette Lundberg: California, 1851*
4. *Mary Alice Peale: Philadelphia, 1777*
5. *Willow Chase: Kansas Territory, 1847*
6. *Ellen Elizabeth Hawkins: Texas, 1886*
7. *Evie Peach: Missouri, 1857*
8. *Celou Sudden Shout: Idaho, 1827*
9. *Summer MacCleary: Virginia, 1720*

Series: Dear America

Author: Different author for each title

Publisher: Scholastic

Each book in this series is presented as the actual diary of the narrator. The books are small, slightly weathered, and even have a bookmark attached. The diary entries capture the personal thoughts of the narrator in her own words. Each book in the series really does recreate a particular time in American history.

Titles: *A Journey to the New World: The Diary of Remember Patience Whipple*, by Kathryn Lasky

The Winter of Red Snow: The Revolutionary War Diary of Abigail Jane Stewart, by Kristiana Gregory

When Will This Cruel War Be Over?: The Civil War Diary of Emma Simpson, by Barry Denenberg

Across the Wild and Lonesome Prairie: The Oregon Trail Diary of Hattie Campbell, by Kristiana Gregory

A Picture of Freedom: The Diary of Clotee, a Slave Girl, by Patricia C. McKissack

I Thought My Soul Would Rise and Fly: The Diary of Patsy, a Freed Girl, by Joyce Hansen

So Far from Home: The Diary of Mary Driscoll, an Irish Mill Girl, by Barry Denenberg

Series: Portraits of Little Women

Author: Pfeffer, Susan Beth

Publisher: Delacorte Press

Here is a treat for all of the fans who enjoyed reading about the March family daughters in Louisa May Alcott's Little Women books. Pfeffer has taken these endearing characters and given them new experiences to share with an audience that is ready for some new stories.

Titles: *Meg's Story*
Jo's Story
Beth's Story
Amy's Story

Series: Her Story

Author: Hoobler, Dorothy, and Thomas Hoobler

Publisher: Silver Burdett Press

Slices of American history are brought to life in these stories about young girls who lived in the different times. The books capture the mood, the difficulties, and the triumphs that were experienced by children who helped in the formation of the country.

Titles: *The Sign Painter's Secret: The Story of a Revolutionary Girl*
Aloha Means Come Back: The Story of a World War II Girl
The Trail on Which They Wept: The Story of a Cherokee Girl
Sally Bradford: The Story of a Rebel Girl
Julie Meyer: The Story of a Wagon Train Girl
Priscilla Foster: The Story of a Salem Girl
Florence Robinson: The Story of a Jazz Age Girl

The Authors' All-Time Favorite Historical Fiction Stories

Avi—**The True Confessions of Charlotte Doyle**

Curtis, Christopher Paul—**The Watsons Go to Birmingham—1963: A Novel**

Cushman, Karen—**Catherine, Called Birdy**

MacLachlan, Patricia—**Sarah, Plain and Tall**

Paulsen, Gary—**Harris and Me: A Summer Remembered**

Paulsen, Gary—**Nightjohn**

6

Chapter 7

Mysteries

Many of today's children are finding mystery to be their genre of choice. The stories are written so that the readers are involved as the stories develop. Some of the earlier series, like Choose Your Own Adventure or Encyclopedia Brown, guaranteed readers' involvement by having them control the development of the story (for example, by choosing the next page to be read), or by having readers guess the outcome of the mystery, which always had the answer printed upside down on the last page of the book. The stories today hold young people's interest by challenging them to solve the mystery. Readers actively participate by trying to solve a problem that is left as a cliffhanger at the end of each chapter. They work to bring together all the clues that have been sprinkled throughout the story.

Another choice that young mystery readers have today is reading, and writing, mystery stories on the Internet. They can go into interactive book sites and control the development of the stories, just like in the earlier book series, but now the options are limitless when changing the stories' outcomes.

Either way young mystery readers go to "solve the crime," they'll find that their hearts will beat a little faster until they reach each exciting climax. One thing is for certain, though, and that is that the act of reading, and solving, one mystery always leads to reading every other one that can be found. Here are some choices that will keep any mystery reader spellbound and searching for more.

Crime

Crew, Gary
Angel's Gate

Simon & Schuster Books for Young Readers. 1995.   ISBN: 0-689-80166-1. 252 p.

Kimmy and her sister, Julia, saw two children in the truck the day the gold digger, Flannigan, came to have their father treat a bad cut on his arm. When Flannigan is murdered and the children disappear in the hills beyond Angel's Gate, people catch glimpses of them. They are wild children. When they are finally caught, Kimmy tries to befriend and teach Micky and Leena while protecting them from their father's murderer. This mystery, set in Australia, keeps the reader intrigued from beginning to end.

L.W.

Stevenson, James
6-8 The Bones in the Cliff

Greenwillow Books. 1995.   ISBN: 0-688-13745-8. 119 p.

Pete's life has been very strange and confusing. In only eleven years, he has seen his mother drift away until she spends her days in a hospital unable to recognize anyone. His father, an alcoholic, is on the run from a hitman. The only bright spot is his zany new friend, Rootie. Many disturbing and complex issues come to light in this unusual dark novel by James Stevenson, best known for his humorous picture books. The saga continues in the equally dark and disturbing sequel.

Series/Sequels: *The Bones in the Cliff; The Unprotected Witness*

L.W.

Stevenson, James
6-8 The Unprotected Witness

Greenwillow Books. 1997   ISBN: 0-688-15133-7. 176 p.

Pete's father, who was taken into the witness protection program in ***Bones in the Cliff***, was discovered. Now, he has been murdered, and Pete talks directly to the readers about his ordeal in this first person narrative. This is a deeply unsettling sequel to the previous novel that certainly is not meant for everyone. The older readers who choose to read this book will be left with as many questions as they have answers in this very thought-provoking but difficult read.

B.D.V.

Mystery and Detective Stories

Levin, Betty
Island Bound

Greenwillow Books. 1997.   ISBN: 0-688-15217-1. 218 p.

Chris Fossett and Joellen Roth are both on uninhabited Fowler's Island for different reasons: Chris is on a dare to live off the land for one week; Joellen is revisiting a puffin sanctuary started by her father. Eventually the two meet and join forces to solve a mystery involving nineteenth-century Irish immigrants, buried treasure, and a long-lost diary. The book takes a while to get started (the pair doesn't meet until a third of the way into the novel), but the wild setting, interesting relationship between the two headstrong, determined children, and the ecological message should satisfy readers.

C.P.S.

Nixon, Joan Lowery
Search for the Shadowman

Delacorte Press. 1996.   ISBN: 0-385-32203-8. 149 p.

Andy Thomas would never have imagined that his seventh-grade history assignment to explore his family's history could lead to solving a hundred-year-old mystery. The Bonner family disowned Coley Joe Bonner, and Andy believes Coley Joe was accused unfairly. Using every possible avenue, including interviews, the library, and the Internet, Andy uncovers the truth about Coley Joe and clears his name. In addition to giving readers an intriguing mystery, Joan Lowery Nixon has woven a piece of history, the Texas Salt Wars, into the story.

L.W.

Wallace, Barbara Brooks
Cousins in the Castle

Atheneum Books for Young Readers. 1996.   ISBN: 0-689-80637-X. 152 p.

After her father is lost in a terrible accident, Amelia Fairwick must travel to America to meet her new guardian, Cousin Basil. Upon arrival, Amelia is kidnapped by Nanny Dobbins; locked in a cold, rat-infested room; given stale crusts and grease to eat; and left alone to await her fate. But, hark! Amelia escapes and, in a climax filled with sinister characters, plot twists, and coincidences galore, is reunited with her family. This Victorian whodunit is a lot of fun to read and could be just the ticket for adventurous mystery lovers who are up to a challenging read.

C.P.S.

Wright, Betty Ren
Too Many Secrets

Scholastic. 1997.   ISBN: 0-590-25235-6. 116 p.

When Miss Beane hires nine-year-old Chad to walk her dog while she is in the hospital, Chad becomes a self-appointed detective. Miss Beane is recuperating from a twisted ankle incurred while chasing a burglar who had broken into her house. Chad and Jeannie, his eleven-year-old friend, decide to take matters into their own hands and catch the burglar. Initially, they watch the house from the outside. Then, Chad "borrows" the house keys so they can monitor the situation from the inside. Their sleuthing moves to a dangerous level, though, when the burglar returns to the scene. Younger and middle readers alike will be involved in this crime story, while learning about what can happen when the authorities are not contacted and the proper procedures aren't followed.

Series/Sequels: *The Ghost Comes Calling*; *Too Many Secrets*

B.D.V.

Ghosts

W hat better way to begin the section on ghosts than with an eerie collection of short stories by Patricia McKissack. Her stories let the readers slip into a life where everything is not as it seems. They present an unsettling view of African America history. Begin this section with some haunting little tales that pack the weight of a full-blown novel.

McKissack, Patricia C.; Brian Pinkney, illus.
The Dark-Thirty: Southern Tales of the Supernatural

Alfred A. Knopf. 1992   ISBN: 0-679-81863-4. 122p.

Those minutes in the evening when it is not quite dark, yet it isn't daylight, are known as the dark-thirty, the half hour when the ghosts and monsters are said to be on the prowl. This is the best time to tell these spine-tingling tales that leave a lasting grip on the listener. The stories are all based on African American history and range in time from slavery in the 1800s to the Civil Rights Movement. They are filled with ghosts, the supernatural, tricks of the mind, and suspense. McKissack has given middle and upper grade readers some powerful and mysterious tales that leave many unanswered questions. Excellent material for read-alouds.

Awards: ALA Notable Books for Children, 1992; Coretta Scott King Award, 1993; Newbery Award Honor Book, 1993

B.D.V.

Reiss, Kathryn
Time Windows

Harcourt Brace. 1991.   ISBN: 015-288-2057. 272 p.

Moving from the hustle and bustle of New York City to Garnet, Maryland, seems like a dream come true for thirteen-year-old Miranda and her parents, especially because they'll be moving into a gorgeous (if dilapidated) 200-year-old house. Miranda is even happier when she discovers an ornate dollhouse in the attic. Delight soon turns to terror, though, when she learns that this toy is haunted by the spirits of past inhabitants of the house and when she discovers that the house has an ominous effect on her mother. Fans of The Dollhouse Murders will enjoy this good, if slightly long, suspense novel.

C.P.S.

Russell, Barbara Timberlake
Blue Lightning

Viking. 1997.   ISBN: 0-670-87023-4. 122 p.

When twelve-year-old Calvin is hit by lightning while practicing baseball, he is rushed to the hospital, where he has an out-of-body experience and sees his deceased father beckoning to him. Calvin survives the accident, but literally picks up the ghost of Rory, another young baseball enthusiast, who hitchhikes out of the hospital inside Calvin. Rory proceeds to make Calvin's life impossible, until Calvin realizes that there is a spiritual purpose behind the haunting. The blend of sports with the supernatural will make this book popular, yet its pronounced spiritual message might limit its appeal.

C.P.S.

Wright, Betty Ren
Haunted Summer

Scholastic. 1996.   ISBN: 0-590-473557-7. 99 p.

Nine-year-old Abby Tolson finds a strange little chest of drawers, which is also a music box, in some hand-me-downs from her Aunt Sarah. The box seems to play by itself, and an angry young girl in a white cap is seen roaming the house. Abby surprises everyone when she confronts the ghost, who is trying to reclaim the stolen music box. Betty Ren Wright maintains her reputation of writing real page-turners in this mystery, which will be hard to put down.

L.W.

Supernatural

Anderson, Janet S.
Going through the Gate

Dutton Children's Books. 1997.   ISBN: 0-525-45836-0. 134 p.

Every year, Miss Clough's sixth-graders experience a strange graduation ceremony that involves each of them studying an animal in great depth. Even though several generations of students have participated in the mysterious ritual, no one will talk about it except to say that "going through the gate" changes their lives forever. The five sixth-graders who are ready to graduate are surrounded by magic, mystery, and danger as they discover the secret that lies just beyond the gate.

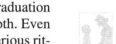

L.W.

Coville, Bruce; Gary A. Lippincott, illus.
The Skull of Truth: A Magic Shop Book

Harcourt Brace. 1997.   ISBN: 0-15-275457-1. 195p.

Charlie is in the sixth grade, and he has not been able to tell the truth since he was a second-grader. When he stumbles into Mr. Elives's Magic Shop, he steals a creepy skull that has the strange power to make people tell the truth. What do you do with a mysterious talking skull who tells you he is Yorick, The Skull of Truth? Everyone's life changes as the truth is told in this story of magic, mystery, and adventure.

Series/Sequels: *Jennifer Mudley's Toad: A Magic Shop Book*; *Jeremy Thatcher, Dragon Hatcher: A Magic Shop Book*; *Skull of Truth: A Magic Shop Book*

L.W.

Lisle, Janet Taylor
A Message from the Match Girl

Orchard. 1995.   ISBN: 0-531-08787-5. 121 p.

Walter is sure that the ghost of his mother, who died when he was just a baby, is trying to contact him. He finds the only known photograph of his mother, and in the background is the statue of the Little Match Girl in Andersen

Park. The mystery begins as he finds a baby mitten, tiny socks, and his hospital brace-let at the base of the statue. Reading this third story about the Investigators of the Un-known, the reader is sure to be intrigued by this puzzling, haunting mystery.

Series/Sequels: Investigators of the Unknown Series: *Gold Dust Letters*; *Looking for Juliette*; *A Message from the Match Girl*; *Angela's Aliens*

L.W.

Lisle, Janet Taylor
Angela's Aliens

Orchard. 1996   ISBN: 0-531-09541-X. 120 p.

The final book in the Investigators of the Unknown series will leave readers with a lot to ponder. Angela has been in Mexico for the past year, and now that she has returned she is almost unrecognizable to her friends. Not only is the new Angela taller, she has become stand offish and aloof to everyone around her. She doesn't even want to spend time with Georgina, her "former" best friend. When Angela mentions that she was abducted by ali-ens while she was away, even her friends don't know what to believe. Lisle has become more introspective in this final novel in the series. Fans will have much more to consider with this twist at the conclusion. A satisfying ending for this thought-provoking series.

Series/Sequels: Investigators of the Unknown Series: *Gold Dust Letters*; *Looking for Juliette*; *A Message from the Match Girl*; *Angela's Aliens*

B.D.V.

Mowry, Jess
6-8 Ghost Train

Henry Holt. 1996.   ISBN: 0-8050-4440-X. 164 p.

At the age of thirteen, Remi is quickly learning that life in Oakland, California—with gangs, crack, and guns—is very different from his life in Haiti. But even more dis-turbing is a ghost train passing by his bedroom window at the same time every night. Remi and his new friend, Niya, set out to solve the mystery of the train and the murder that is reenacted every night. This mature page-turner combines street life in Califor-nia, a murder mystery, and time travel in a thrilling package.

L.W.

Philip Pullman has written an intriguing tale for younger readers in the following story.

Pullman, Philip; Gore, Leonid, illus.
Clockwork

Arthur A. Levine Books. 1998   ISBN: 0-590-12999-6. 112 p.

The story takes place long ago in a small town in Germany where the clock of Glockenheim, the greatest clock in all of Germany, is housed. The clock is filled with figures that seem to come to life whenever the hour is struck, and the townspeople are excited because tomorrow Karl, the clockmaker's apprentice, will add his figure to the clock. To pass the time, Fritz, the storyteller, is about to tell his scariest story yet when he receives some unsettling news from Karl. Coincidentally, Fritz's story is called *Clockwork*, and it is so frightening that even he can't write the conclusion. Pullman brings his great gift of storytelling to younger readers in this fast-paced, rich, and haunting tale that is not to be missed.

B.D.V.

Humor in a Mystery

Byars, Betsy
Tarot Says Beware

Viking. 1995.   ISBN: 0-670-85575-8. 151 p.

Herculeah Jones has "radar hair" that frizzles when something is wrong. The day she notices that Madame Rosa's front door is open and her parrot, Tarot, has flown outside, Herculeah is sure that something is wrong. She soon learns that her neighbor, the eccentric fortune-teller Madame Rosa, has been murdered, and her parrot seems to be the only witness. With the help of her bungling sidekick, Meat, Herculeah tries to track down the killer. There is just enough frightful intrigue to keep younger mystery fans turning the pages as the crime is solved.

Series/Sequels: *Dark Stairs*; *Dead Letter*; *Death's Door*; *Tarot Says Beware*

L.W.

Maguire, Gregory
Seven Spiders Spinning

Houghton. 1994.   ISBN: 0-395-68965-1. 132 p.

Through a chain of improbable comic events, seven lethally poisonous, prehistoric orphan spiders, buried for a zillion years in ice, are accidentally thawed and let loose on a small Vermont town around Halloween. Mistaking a group of nasty girls for their mothers, each baby spider (growing bigger by the minute) goes on a quest to the local elementary school, hoping to catch his "mother" and express devotion by bestowing a love bite. Ouch! This is a breezy, silly story with no ambition other than to entertain. Perfect for readers wanting something funny in a story that hints of mystery. This story makes a great October read-aloud.

C.P.S.

Richler, Mordecai; Michael Chesworth, illus.
Jacob Two-Two's First Spy Case

Farrar, Straus & Giroux. 1997.   ISBN: 0-374-33659-8. 152 p.

It's hard to make anyone listen to you when you are the youngest child in a big family. Jacob Two-Two has to say everything twice before he's even heard—that's how he got his name. In this third Jacob Two-Two story, Jacob enlists the aid of his mysterious neighbor, Mr. Dinglebat, to help him learn the secrets about Perfectly Loathsome Leo Louse and the dreadful school lunch program. The humor is very slapstick in this madcap mystery for young readers.

Series/Sequels: *Jacob Two-Two and the Dinosaur*; *Jacob Two-Two Meets the Hooded Fang*; *Jacob Two-Two's First Spy Case*

L.W.

Paperback Mystery and Horror Series

Since the success of the Goosebumps series, publishers have been quick to get new mystery series to readers. Here are some that are popular and in print at this time, but the market is constantly changing in this area. Be sure to check with your local library, bookstores, and the Internet to learn about the newest titles.

The Baby-Sitters Mystery series is listed with the Baby-Sitters Club series in the Contemporary Life chapter, (p. 82).

Series: Bone Chillers

> Author: Haynes, Betsy, creator; various authors
>
> Publisher: Harper Paperbacks

This series does exactly what its name proposes: it is made up of scary and exciting stories to chill the bones of readers. Like Goosebumps, a different group of characters in each book works to solve the mysteries that are presented in the story, with very little help from adults. A Saturday morning program of this series can be seen on ABC television.

Titles:
1. *Beware the Shopping Mall*
2. *Little Pet Shop of Horrors*
3. *Back to School*
4. *Frankenturkey*
5. *Strange Brew*
6. *Teacher Creature*
7. *Frankenturkey II*
8. *Welcome to Alien Inn*
9. *Attack of the Killer Ants*
10. *Slime Time*
11. *Toilet Terror*
12. *Night of the Living Clay*
13. *The Thing Under the Bed*
14. *A Terminal Case of the Uglies*
15. *Tiki Doll of Doom*
16. *The Queen of the Gargoyles*
17. *Why I Quit the Baby-sitters Club*
18. *Blowtorch@psycho.com*
19. *The Night Squawker*
20. *Scare-Bear*
21. *The Dog Ate My Homework*
22. *Killer Clown of King's County*

Series: Deadtime Stories

Author: Cascone, A. G.

Publisher: Troll Medallion

The Deadtime Stories series is actually written by two sisters who work together to create these chilling tales for younger readers. The stories are written in the same vein as Goosebumps, but they are easier to share with the younger crowd.

Titles: 1.   *Terror in Tiny Town*
      2.   *Invasion of the Appleheads*
      3.   *Along Came a Spider*
      4.   *Ghost Knight*
      5.   *Revenge of the Goblins*
      6.   *Little Magic Shop of Horrors*
      7.   *It Came from the Deep*
      8.   *Grave Secrets*
      9.   *Mirror, Mirror*
     10.   *Grandpa's Monster Movies*
     11.   *Nightmare on Planet X*
     12.   *Welcome to the Terror-Go-Round*
     13.   *Beast of Baskerville*
     14.   *Trapped in Tiny Town*
     15.   *Cyber Scare*
     16.   *Night of the Pet Zombies*
     17.   *Faerie Tale*

Series: Goosebumps

Author: Stine, R. L.

Publisher: Scholastic

Here is the series that has become a household word throughout the country. Kids find themselves in eerie and sometimes frightful situations in each one of these ghoulish stories. Somehow, the characters always reach a happy resolution by the end of each tale. A television series based on these titles appears on the Fox Network on Saturday mornings.

Titles: 1.   *Welcome to Dead House*
      2.   *Stay Out of the Basement*
      3.   *Monster Blood*
      4.   *Say Cheese and Die*
      5.   *The Curse of the Mummies Tomb*
      6.   *Let's Get Invisible!*
      7.   *Night of the Living Dummy*
      8.   *The Girl Who Cried Monster*
      9.   *Welcome to Camp Nightmare*

10. *The Ghost Next Door*
11. *The Haunted Mask*
12. *Be Careful What You Wish for ...*
13. *Piano Lessons Can Be Murder*
14. *The Werewolf of Fever Swamp*
15. *You Can't Scare Me!*
16. *One Day at Horrorland*
17. *Why I'm Afraid of Bees*
18. *Monster Blood 2*
19. *Deep Trouble*
20. *The Scarecrow Walks at Midnight*
21. *Go Eat Worms!*
22. *Ghost Beach*
23. *Return of the Mummy*
24. *Phantom of the Auditorium*
25. *Attack of the Mutant*
26. *My Hairiest Adventure*
27. *A Night in Terror Tower*
28. *The Cuckoo Clock of Doom*
29. *Monster Blood 3*
30. *It Came from Beneath the Sink!*
31. *Night of the Living Dummy 2*
32. *The Barking Ghost*
33. *The Horror at Camp Jellyjam*
34. *Revenge of the Lawn Gnomes*
35. *A Shocker on Shock Street*
36. *The Haunted Mask 2*
37. *The Headless Ghost*
38. *The Abominable Snowman of Pasadena*
39. *How I Got My Shrunken Head*
40. *Night of the Living Dummy 3*
41. *Bad Hare Day*
42. *Egg Monsters from Mars*
43. *The Beast from the East*
44. *Say Cheese and Die—Again!*
45. *Ghost Camp*
46. *How to Kill a Monster*
47. *Legend of the Lost Legend*
48. *Attack of the Jack O Lanterns*
49. *Vampire Breath*
50. *Calling All Creeps!*
51. *Beware, the Snowman*
52. *How I Learned to Fly*
53. *Chicken Chicken*

54. *Don't Go to Sleep*
55. *The Blob that Ate Everyone*
56. *The Curse of Camp Cold Lake*
57. *My Best Friend Is Invisible*
58. *Deep Trouble II*
59. *The Haunted School*
60. *Werewolf Skin*
61. *I Live in Your Basement!*

Since the success of the Goosebumps series, there have been two spinoffs
that have been just as popular as the original.

Series: Give Yourself Goosebumps

Author: Stine, R. L.

Publisher: Scholastic

Titles: 1. *Escape from the Carnival*
2. *Tick, Tock, You're Dead*
3. *Trapped in Bat Wing Hall*
4. *The Deadly Experiments*
5. *Night in Werewolf Woods*
6. *Beware the Purple Peanut Butter*
7. *Under the Magician's Spell*
8. *The Curse of the Creeping Coffin*
9. *The Night in Screaming Armour*
10. *Diary of a Mad Mummy*
11. *Deep in the Jungle of Doom*
12. *Welcome to the Wicked Wax Museum*
13. *Scream of the Evil Genie*
14. *The Creepy Creations of Professor Shock*
15. *Please Don't Feed the Vampire*
16. *Secret Agent Grandma*
17. *The Little Comic Shop of Horrors*
18. *Attack of the Beastly Baby-sitter*
19. *Escape from Camp, Run for Your Life*
20. *Toy Terror, Batteries Included*
21. *The Twisted Tale of Tiki Island*
22. *Return to the Carnival of Horrors*
23. *Zapped in Space*
24. *Lost in Stinkeye*
25. *Shop Till You Drop—Dead*
26. *Alone in Snakebite Canyon*
27. *Checkout Time at the Dead-end Hotel*

Series: Goosebumps 2000

Author: Stine, R. L.

Publisher: Scholastic

Titles: 1. *Cry of the Cat*
2. *Bride of the Living Dummy*
3. *Creature Teacher*
4. *Invasion of the Body Squeezers, Pt. 1*
5. *Invasion of the Body Squeezers, Pt. 2*

Series: Graveyard School

Author: Stone, Tom B.

Publisher: Bantam Books

Vicki, Maria, and Stacey are sixth-graders who attend Grove Hill Elementary School, commonly referred to as Graveyard School. This name came about because of the graveyard that is located up the hill, behind the school. Strange things are happening at Grove Hill, though, and the three girls are always involved in the bizarre activities there.

Titles: 1. *Don't Eat the Mystery Meat!*
2. *The Skeleton on the Skateboard*
3. *The Headless Bicycle Rider*
4. *Little Pet Werewolf*
5. *Revenge of the Dinosaurs*
6. *Camp Dracula*
7. *Slime Lake*
8. *Let's Scare the Teacher to Death!*
9. *The Abominable Snow Monster*
10. *There's a Ghost in the Boys' Bathroom*
11. *April Ghouls' Day*
12. *Scream, Team!*
13. *Tales Too Scary to Tell at Camp*
14. *Tragic School Bus*
15. *Fright Before Christmas*
16. *Don't Tell Mummy*
17. *Jack and the Beanstalker*
18. *Dead Sox*
19. *Gator Ate Her*
20. *Creature Teacher*
21. *Skeleton's Revenge*
22. *Boo Year's Eve*
23. *Easter Egg Haunt*

Series: The Internet Detectives

Author: Coleman, Michael

Publisher: Skylark Books

Here is a new mystery series for those who love to work with computers. Tamsyn, Rob, and Josh solve crimes by sending e-mail messages to each other and to other mystery buffs around the world. There are several pages with computer screen shots, to make readers feel that they are right there, which heightens the excitement.

Titles:
1. *Net Bandits*
2. *Escape Key*
3. *Speed Surf*
4. *Cyber Feud*

Series: Spooksville

Author: Pike, Christopher

Publisher: Pocket Books

The town is called Spooksville, and terrifying events seem to take place there on a regular basis. A gang of twelve-year-olds—Adam, Sally, Cindy, Bryce, Watch, and sometimes Tira and George—has formed to battle against the mysterious happenings and frightful creatures that are invading their town.

Titles:
1. *The Secret Path*
2. *The Howling Ghost*
3. *The Haunted Cave*
4. *Aliens in the Sky*
5. *The Cold People*
6. *The Witch's Revenge*
7. *The Dark Corner*
8. *The Little People*
9. *The Wishing Stone*
10. *The Wicked Cat*
11. *The Deadly Past*
12. *The Hidden Beast*
13. *Creature in the Teacher*
14. *The Evil House*
15. *Invasion of the No-Ones*
16. *Time Terror*
17. *The Thing in the Closet*
18. *Attack of the Killer Crabs*
19. *Night of the Vampire*
20. *The Dangerous Quest*
21. *Living Dead*

Series: Stevie Diamond Mysteries

> Author: Bailey, Linda
>
> Publisher: Albert Whitman

Stevie Diamond, along with her best friend and partner Jessie Kulniki, set out to solve the quirky mysteries that come their way. These episodes are filled not only with unusual plots, but also with humorous dialogue and endearing characters that add to the fun in solving the mysteries.

> Titles: 1.   *How Come the Best Clues Are Always in the Garbage?*
> 2.   *How Can I Be a Detective if I Have to Baby-sit?*
> 3.   *Who's Got Gertie? And How Can We Get Her Back?*
> 4.   *How Can a Frozen Detective Stay Hot on the Trail?*
> 5.   *What's a Daring Detective Like Me Doing in the Doghouse?*

Series: Strange Matter

> Author: Engle, Marty M., and Johnny Ray Barnes
>
> Publisher: Montage

Here is another scary series, with some wit and catchy dialogue, for readers looking for more books of chilling tales. The children in this series come from the town of Fairfield, where many strange occurrences take place. It is up to these characters to figure out a way to escape from these strange situations.

> Titles: 1.   *No Substitutions*
> 2.   *The Midnight Game*
> 3.   *Driven to Death*
> 4.   *A Place to Hide*
> 5.   *The Last One In*
> 6.   *Bad Circuits*
> 7.   *Fly the Unfriendly Skies*
> 8.   *Frozen Dinners*
> 9.   *Deadly Delivery*
> 10.   *Knightmare*
> 11.   *Something Rotten*
> 12.   *Dead on Its Tracks*
> 13.   *Toy Trouble*
> 14.   *Plant People*
> 15.   *Creature Features*
> 16.   *The Weird Weird West*
> 17.   *Tune in to Terror*
> 18.   *The Fairfield Triangle*
> 19.   *Bigfoot, Big Trouble*
> 20.   *Doorway to Doom*
> 21.   *Under Wraps*

The Authors' All-Time Favorite Mystery and Horror Stories

Howe, James—**Bunnicula**

Mahy, Margaret—**The Haunting**

Naylor, Phyllis Reynolds—**Witch's Sister**

Naylor, Phyllis Reynolds—**Witch Water**

Naylor, Phyllis Reynolds—**The Witch Herself**

Naylor, Phyllis Reynolds—**The Witch's Eye**

Naylor, Phyllis Reynolds—**Witch Weed**

Raskin, Ellen—**The Westing Game**

Snyder, Zilpha Keatley—**The Headless Cupid**

Author/Title Index

This index also includes illustrators and series titles.

Subject Index